FATHER TED HESBURGH
HE COACHED ME

FATHER TED HESBURGH
HE COACHED ME

Digger Phelps with Tim Bourret

TRIUMPH
B O O K S

This book is available in quantity at special discounts for your group or organization. For further information, contact:

Triumph Books LLC
814 North Franklin Street
Chicago, Illinois 60610
(312) 337-0747
www.triumphbooks.com

Printed in U.S.A.
ISBN: 978-1-62937-473-4
Design and page production by Heath Bradley

CONTENTS

ACKNOWLEDGEMENTS

Special thanks to Linda Costas for her help in editing of this book and to Karen Blackman for her many hours of transcription. And to Heath Bradley for his layout and design contributions. Cover photo by Brother Charles McBride, University of Notre Dame Sports Information. Interior photos by Digger Phelps, Linda Costas, Chuck Bourret, University of Notre Dame Public Relations and University of Notre Dame archives, Carl Ackerman, Notre Dame Sports Information, Diane Crawford, The United States Postal Service, and Barbara Johnson, Unviversity of Notre Dame Multimedia Services.

INTRODUCTION

Father Ted Hesburgh was a living saint.

That is the most direct way I can say it.

He had an incredible impact on my life, not only when I was the head basketball coach at Notre Dame for 20 years (1971-91), but even more so when I retired. Living to this day just a couple of blocks from campus made it so easy to visit him in his office on the 13th floor of the Hesburgh Library.

You probably don't see a lot of coaches say such things about the presidents they worked for, especially over a 20-year period, but that was the case for me.

I learned so much from him through the examples he set. They led to lessons I passed on to my players. Today I am proud of all of my former players and their contributions to society. Our approach was one where our program was bigger than just basketball.

That all came from Father Ted.

But, for me personally, he inspired me spiritually.

Whether they were dinners at Parisi's Restaurant in South Bend or two-hour conversations in his office, I wanted to share the stories of his influence on my life. That is why I wrote this book.

I was a part of Father Hesburgh's life journey for 44 years. I know how fortunate I was to have him as the Notre Dame President when I came here in 1971. Whenever I went to his office with a problem, you just knew he was going to provide you with a sound recommendation.

I am one of many who benefitted from knowing Father Hesburgh. Other than Father Edward Sorin, who founded the University of Notre Dame in 1842, Father Hesburgh is the key person in the history of this institution.

Father Ted told me he wanted to become a priest when he was six and he came to Notre Dame at the age of 16. That was his mission in life, to be a priest. In his 35 years as president, he made this the top Catholic institution of higher learning in the world.

While his mission was to simply be a priest, he was so much more to so many people. I discuss his impact on the world through many stories he told about his involvement on the Civil Rights Commission for 15 years, one of 16 presidential appointments he held.

He was a man with great people skills and integrity and he applied those skills every day in the way he ran the University with the help of Father Edmund P. Joyce.

So, he inspired me to become more than a basketball coach. And at the same time, this book shares what I learned from him, what he valued, what he believed, and what he wanted to be done by all of us.

Hopefully the examples of his inspiration of me will inspire others to make changes in this world today for people who have not been so blessed.

As Mother Teresa was as a nun, Father Ted was as a priest. I certainly hope one day Father Ted follows her into Sainthood.

—Digger Phelps

As a Notre Dame student from 1973-78, I benefitted from the wisdom of Father Hesburgh. I first met him when I was 10 years old at a Notre Dame Alumni Club meeting in Hartford, Connecticut. My father was class of '48 and I was told about the great leader of his alma mater at an early age.

I had great respect for Father Hesburgh and what he did for the school while I was a student, but that only continued to grow as I entered the working world in South Carolina as sports information director at Clemson University.

When I traveled the country as part of my job and visited various universities, I could sense the respect people had for Notre Dame. And to me that great respect was a result of the way Father Hesburgh represented the school and showed an ability to convey those central values to Notre Dame students and graduates.

For those of us that graduated and moved away, there was a sense of carrying on the Notre Dame mission throughout the country. There was a sense of service.

As I come to the end of my career, I felt an urge to thank Notre Dame and Father Hesburgh for having such a positive impact on my life and for opening so many doors. When I applied for my first job at Clemson in 1978, Notre Dame's athletic reputation and reputation for producing outstanding administrators helped my chances in being hired. Forty years later I am still here. Clemson has been great to me, but I owe the opportunity I had to Notre Dame.

And that reputation, even in the college athletic world is not traced back to a former student-athlete, or even a great coach like Digger Phelps. That reputation for excellence is traced back to Father Hesburgh.

My second reason for doing this book is my relationship with Digger Phelps. I wanted people to see another side of Coach Phelps through his relationship with perhaps the most important American priest in the last 100 years.

I also wanted Notre Dame people to understand the degree to which Coach Phelps cares about this school and the people who made it great.

—**Tim Bourret**

CHAPTER 1
THE FINAL WEEK

On Tuesday, February 24, 2015 one of my former managers at Notre Dame, Mike Gurdak, a lawyer in Washington, D.C., went on one of the internet sites that covers Notre Dame and saw someone had posted that Father Ted Hesburgh was gravely ill.

So I called him. "Mike, that's not true," I said because I just didn't want to hear that. I didn't want to face it.

I immediately called Melanie Chapleau, who had served as Father Ted's office assistant the last 28 years. "What's going on with Father Ted?" She said, "Well, he's okay, but he's over at the Holy Cross House."

There were times when Father Ted had health issues, but after a week or two, he would bounce back and would be good for six months.

But in the winter he had to hibernate to some degree. He just couldn't go many places because of the South Bend weather. Once in a while, Melanie and others would take him to his office across campus on the 13th floor of the library named in his honor.

So, that day I went to the 11:30 a.m. Mass at Holy Cross House, which is where most of the priests live. That is the time they concelebrate mass each weekday. As he was coming in with his nurse in a wheelchair, I put my hand out, leaned down and said, "Fr. Ted, it's Digger."

He said to me, "Pray for me."

That hit me, It was the first time in 44 years he said that to me. I still tear up today when I think about him saying that to me. I had asked him to pray for me many times and he had given me special blessings and guidance when I was going through prostate and bladder cancer within the last six years.

I got myself together and said, "That's why I am here."

He went up front with the other priests where he always sat to concelebrate the Mass.

After Mass, I waited for him and said, "I said prayers for you today."

I then said, "Please, give me a blessing!" So he took his thumb and blessed me on the forehead.

He went into the cafeteria and I spoke with Jim and Mary, his brother and sister-in-law in the hallway outside.

All of a sudden the nurse came out and said to me, "He wants to talk to you. Come inside."

So I went inside and sat down at his table next to him. Father Don McNeill was sitting there also and when I sat down, Father Don said to Father Hesburgh, "Oh, you've got the coach that beat UCLA here to see you."

"Forget UCLA," I said. "Father Ted was 7-0 on our bench. Remember when we beat No. 1 DePaul in double overtime, Father? He was there for that one too."

3

I went into my pep talk mode.

"We're going to win this." He said, "Win what?"

I said, "This game with your health. We have to keep you strong and keep praying. You're going to be fine. The weather is bad now, but it is going to get better. We just need to get you to the spring. You just have to take care and make sure you're eating and keeping your strength up."

I then said, "By the way, your hometown team beat Notre Dame last night."

Father Hesburgh was from Syracuse, NY and Jim Boeheim's team had beaten the Irish the previous night in an upset at Notre Dame. He replied, "I heard that."

We visited for about 20 minutes. His mind was still sharp and he knew what was going on. That was a good sign to me, but I decided I wanted to go to this Mass every day and see him.

The next day, Wednesday Feb. 25, 2015, I went back to the 11:30 a.m. service. I had gone to these Masses before through Jim Gibbons, who worked for Father Hesburgh in many capacities in public relations, event planning and fund raising. He was a student-athlete, baseball and basketball coach in the 1950s and 1960s, then went into administration.

He is a Notre Dame institution.

Now retired, he still came to these Masses each day and served as a defacto altar boy, assisting the priests with the various duties during the Mass. The only other people there besides the priests were members of Father Hesburgh's family.

On this day, I told Father Ted that Linda (Costas) my fiancée, whom he knew, said hello. After Mass I again went into the dining room and sat next to him.

"You're the Godfather of the Civil Rights Act," I said. "You're the one who got me coaching the streets."

He smiled and said to me, "I want you to keep coaching the streets." He was still motivating me. That was his mission with so many. He was the master motivator over the years, but more on that later.

He just sat and looked from his wheelchair at the table. I continued the conversation.

"Remember when I came to get a blessing before my bladder cancer surgery? After you blessed me before the bladder cancer surgery you said, 'Digger, have the courage.'

I always remembered that and keep that note in my wallet to this day."

Have the courage.

Keeping that note makes me feel like Fr. Hesburgh is there with me. On this day, I wanted him to know that.

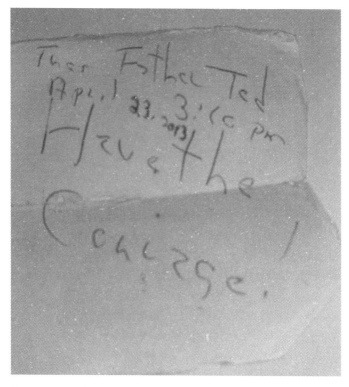

I keep a piece of paper with me at all times that reminds me what Father Ted told me when I found out I had cancer in 2013.

So, I said to him before I left, "Father Ted, have the courage."

As I left I just kept thinking he would be OK. It didn't seem like anything specifically was wrong. He just had a cold like he had before and was a little down. I still kept positive and believed he would get through it.

On Wednesday night, Linda asked if she

could go to the Thursday Mass. I thought about it and said, "Sure, I will pick you up from work." Linda has a position in Notre Dame administration in human resources.

I still remember the first time I brought Linda to meet Father Ted in his office on the 13th floor of the Hesburgh Library.

Linda is Jewish, but she knew all about Fr. Hesburgh and his legacy as Notre Dame's longest serving president from 1952-87 and his impact on civil rights in this country.

When we walked in, Fr. Hesburgh was behind his desk smoking a Cuban cigar. I didn't know if it was one of the cigars I had gotten him, but I always tried to keep him stocked. Smoking a good Cuban cigar was one his private passions.

One of the first things I said that day as I looked out his office window at the Blessed Mother on the Golden Dome was, "Mary was Jewish. Jesus was Jewish. Mary Magdalene was Jewish. Linda is Jewish. Linda is my Mary Magdalene."

He started looking at me with a "Where are you going with this?" expression.

"Father, they were all Jewish back then."

He went to her and blessed her on the forehead and said, "You're going to need that with this guy."

She thought she had just met the Pope and

didn't wash her forehead for three days.

You talk about things happening for a reason at a certain place and time! There are spiritual powers.

We arrived at the chapel on Thursday morning and Fr. Ted came in the door in his wheelchair at that exact moment. I said, "Father, it's Digger and I have Linda here today."

He could hardly see because he was limited by macular degeneration, but he could see the shadow of her figure. He said to her, "Give me a kiss." He kissed her right on the lips. I told his brother Jim and Mary Hesburgh, who were sitting in the last row, "He's fine, he's kissing Linda on the lips."

When Linda sat down, she started to cry and said, "After I kissed him he asked me to pray for him."

That was one of the great ironies of that last day. One of the last persons Fr. Hesburgh kissed was Jewish.

That day after mass, Fr. Ted didn't go to the dining room. He went straight upstairs. He was too sick to eat.

That night, around 2 a.m. I woke up and could not sleep. I couldn't stop thinking about Fr. Ted.

Linda woke up also and looked at e-mail on her cell phone. One of her e-mails said that Father Ted had passed away. I checked my cell phone and sure enough Melanie had called me a little after 11:30 p.m. to give me the difficult news.

"Hi Digger, it's Melanie. Father Ted died tonight about 11:30 pm. I just thought I would let you and Linda know."

I still have that message on my phone.

It was one of those moments that you just don't want to believe, you don't want to accept.

Obviously, I couldn't get to sleep because I was just thinking about all he had done for Notre Dame and for me personally. There was a Sports Illustrated story on Notre Dame athletics during the 1980s and much of it centered around Father Hesburgh and Father Edmond Joyce, who was the executive vice president in control of athletics. They worked together for 35 years. The article was entitled "Casting a Special Light." That's what Hesburgh had been to me since I first came to campus in 1971. He had been my guiding light for 44 years.

Over night students gathered at the Grotto. They lit candles and placed them in a formation at the left wing of the grotto that spelled "Ted". Later many other students locked arms and sang the alma mater (you can watch it on Youtube).

The local news had live reports from campus early in the morning with reaction from students, staff and faculty. There were

Notre Dame students honored Father Hesburgh by lighting candles at the Grotto spelling "TED" in the early morning hours of 2/27/2015.

expressions of sorrow from leaders from all over the country. A resolution was adopted on the floor of the House and Senate, a movement led by Senator Joe Donnelly from Indiana, a Notre Dame graduate.

Donnelly was also one of 12 speakers at a memorial service for Father Hesburgh in the Athletic and Convocation Center's Purcell Pavilion the night of the funeral. The other speakers included Dr. Condoleezza Rice and former President Jimmy Carter.

I went to Mass Friday at Holy Cross House and it was therapeutic in that it was all about giving thanks for Father Ted's life and what he had meant to all these priests. It occurred to me and many of the priests at that Mass, that Father

Ted had done something on his last day of life that he always wished for.

He told many that he wanted to say Mass on his last day of life. No matter where he was in the world, he said Mass every day. He had done that as a concelebrant on his last day, and I was privileged to be there.

I spent much of the weekend doing interviews about Father Hesburgh's incredible life, legacy and my personal reflections. All three local television stations, University of Notre Dame media, the South Bend Tribune and others asked for my reflection on Father Ted's life. I held it together for most of the time, but had to take a break a few times when I was overcome with emotion. But, it was good to talk about him and get my emotions out.

The Wake

Tuesday, March 3, 2015 was the wake at Sacred Heart Basilica. He was to lie in state in front of the altar for 24 hours. The constant procession of people from all walks of life was incredible. The media estimated that 12,000 people came through Sacred Heart during the 24 hours.

Linda and I were there at 3 pm on Tuesday when they brought the casket in. We entered from the right side of the church, the entrance nearest the Golden Dome (Administration building).

It was an open casket and as soon as I saw Fr. Ted I just lost it. I must have cried hysterically for 10 minutes. Seeing him in that state was just such a shock. He is gone. It just struck me so sharply. He had been such an influence on me, professionally, personally and spiritually. And I was just one of so many on this campus that followed his example. Just like there were disciples of Jesus, I was a disciple of Hesburgh.

The way I coached, the work I have done in the streets, that all came from Hesburgh. And he had that impact on so many people around the world.

Father Hesburgh and I talked many hours about one of the unique aspects of Jesus's life was that there were women involved throughout. There was Mary of Bethlehem, his mother, and Mary Magdalene, the woman from Magdala, who was there for his crucifixion and resurrection. So the life of Jesus, he was surrounded by two women, both named Mary.

At his death there were three women, Mary, wife of Clopas, Mary, the Mother of Jesus, and Mary Magdalene.

At Father Hesburgh's death, there were three women, Micki Kidder, Associate Vice President and Executive Director of Development, Breyan Tornifolio, who works in the Notre Dame administration, and Katherine Lane, Senior Director of Special Events and Stewardship.

Breyan was around the casket and Katherine was ushering the family members during the wake. Micki was in many ways in charge of the entire operation from the university standpoint. They were all a major part of all the services. Father Hesburgh would have been proud.

Father Hesburgh loved a good Cuban Cigar so I called Father Austin Collins, who was a close friend of Father Ted's and was a big part of the organization of the wake and the funeral. He had gone to Cuba previously and brought Father Hesburgh back some Cuban cigars. Even in his final days he found a way to find a quiet place to smoke one now and then.

I told Austin, "You have to put one of those Cuban cigars in the casket with him." So, just before they brought Father Ted to the Basilica for the wake, Father Collins put one of those cigars in his left sleeve coat pocket.

After I spent my final moments with Father Ted at the wake, I ran into John Zack, who runs the Basilica. I had two medals, the St. Jude medal and Mary on the Dome, Father Hesburgh had blessed both for me. I said, "Take these two medals and put them with him in the casket, because he blessed them."

I saw John the next day before the funeral Mass and said, "Don't let me down with those medals?" He told me, "They are in there….right next to the cigar."

The Funeral

When we had a big game coming up or after a big win over a top team I referred to them as "Notre Dame Moments." The Hesburgh Funeral, the entire day, was "The Notre Dame Moment."

The sanctity of the service, with 115 members of the clergy, including six bishops as well as Cardinal Theodore McCarrick, archbishop emeritus of Washington, D.C, and Cardinal Roger Mahony, archbishop emeritus of Los Angeles, was so memorable. It was a service in a perfect place, Sacred Heart Basilica, that represented the true spirit of Notre Dame. It was just a perfect way to honor Father Hesburgh.

Dignitaries attending the service ranged from politicians and civic leaders to Notre Dame coaches and benefactors. Leaders of the Congregation of Holy Cross also attended. Fr. Richard V. Warner, superior general of the Congregation, came from Rome, and Fr. Thomas J. O'Hara, provincial superior of the U.S. province of the Congregation, was the principal celebrant.

All classes after 12:20 p.m. were cancelled so the students could view the 2 p.m. service from the DeBartolo Auditorium. Many of them watched, but many lined up on the procession route to the Holy Cross Community Cemetery.

For those of us at the funeral or the 10,000 that went to the memorial service at the Joyce Athletic Center that night, it gave closure. For me that closure came at the wake when I saw him in the casket.

Father John I. Jenkins, the current Notre Dame President, gave the eulogy during the service and Jim Hesburgh made some remarks on behalf of the family at the end of the service. It lasted an hour and 40 minutes.

Jenkins said Father Hesburgh would be remembered for four areas of his leadership because he was a great American and a great citizen of the world.

"How can we draw together the strands of a life that spanned so many years, served in so many realms, and touched so many lives?" Fr. Jenkins said.

"Fr. Ted gave us the answer. He was, first and foremost, a priest. That vocation drove him to build a great Catholic university, it gave his work in the public life its moral focus, it shaped his generosity in all his personal interactions.

"Fr. Ted often spoke of a priest as a pontifex, a Latin word that translates as 'bridge builder.' He modeled this role of a priest who builds bridges between people to draw them together to serve the common good and builds a bridge between human beings and God.

"But the most important thing he gave us at Notre Dame was the vision to be a great Catholic research university and the confidence to realize that dream. In all he did, Fr. Ted's leadership sought to strengthen Notre Dame into a truly great, truly Catholic university."

Fr. Jenkins' eulogy also summarized many of the events of Fr. Hesburgh's public leadership, including his work on behalf of the Civil Rights Movement, immigration, nuclear arms and human suffering.

"His work in the public realm was driven by moral concerns about civil and human rights, peace and serving the needs of the poorest. He was often regarded as the conscience of the bodies on which he served."

Lastly, Jenkins spoke of the acts of kindness that Hesburgh demonstrated on everyone he met, actions that often went unheralded, but will be forever remembered by each individual.

"They are among the reasons, he is not only celebrated, but beloved," Fr. Jenkins said.

Father Jenkins then spoke of the situation he was in during the spring of 2009 when he invited President Barack Obama to campus for commencement. There was much criticism of the decision and Father Hesburgh had heard that Father Jenkins' mother was upset. So without telling Father Jenkins, Father Ted called his mother to calm her concerns.

Jim Hesburgh thanked the Notre Dame family for its outpouring of appreciation for his life. He told of one of Father Ted's axioms of life: "Mediocrity is not how we honor Our Lady."

"Today we celebrate his life, and all that we had for so long taken for granted with Ted suddenly comes into focus."

The decorations in the Basilica were simple, in line with Fr. Ted's wishes to have a normal funeral for a Holy Cross religious.

The Procession and Internment

The most memorable part of the day was the procession from Sacred Heart to the cemetery. All Notre Dame priests are buried on campus and the graves are there with a small head stone. The markers are in order of passing and Fr. Hesburgh's is no bigger than any other priest.

They date to the mid 1880s. Every priest, not just Hesburgh, receives the procession from Sacred Heart to the cemetery.

But, obviously this was special because of the number of people in attendance and for many other reasons.

Marty Ogren had driven Fr. Ted everywhere for years and fittingly he was driving the hearse that brought him to the cemetery.

As we walked out of the basilica down

the hill and past the Grotto we could see that students had lined the street on both sides.

Father Hesburgh once said, "The greatest gift a university president can give his students is the example of his life." Seeing all those students lining the procession route told me the students certainly had received that gift.

But one thing stood out to me. There were many more women than men. I said to Linda, "I thought we were coed?"

I was shocked at the number of women who had come to line up and pay their respects. I got tears in my eyes as we walked passed them.

This was Father Hesburgh's dream. He had made the decision to add women to the student body in 1970, but it had taken until 1972 to get it done. There was an attempt to combine the St. Mary's Community with Notre Dame, but it was just too difficult to make it work. The only thing to do was admit women to Notre Dame. Today each freshman class of approximately 2000 is composed of 50 percent men and 50 percent women.

All these women knew that story and knew Hesburgh's desire to change Notre Dame's long standing policy was the reason they were there. Many of the women there were the product of a marriage between Notre Dame parents who met on campus. That would not have happened if Father Ted had not admitted women.

He had not been Notre Dame's president since 1987, but every one of them knew the impact he had on their education, and the spirit of Notre Dame.

As we got closer to the cemetery there were Navy ROTC members in full uniform standing at attention.

That was another tribute to Hesburgh's legacy. In the spring of 1943 Notre Dame's enrollment had dropped 20 percent from what it was in the fall of 1940 and was just six students larger than what it was in 1933-34 when the depression was still an ongoing factor.

But The US Navy decided to establish a Navy College Training Program at Notre Dame. That added 1,851 trainees to the Notre Dame student population. The Navy paid for nearly $500,000 worth of facilities enhancements and gave the University $9,000 a month to cover heat, light and athletic field maintenance expenses.

"All I can say is without the Navy during the war, this institution would have gotten down to a few hundred students," Hesburgh said during an interview two years before his death. "Instead of that, we were almost twice our normal size during the war."

Additionally, Hesburgh always wanted to be part of the Navy. When he was ordained in 1943, he made it clear to his family that his goal was to be a chaplain on a Navy submarine.

At the conclusion of the service at the cemetery Jim Hesburgh gave Linda and me two roses to remember the service and Father Ted. That is a remembrance I will keep the rest of my life.

Two months after the funeral, I was driving on campus and saw Jim again. I rolled down the window and he simply said, "Do you miss him?" And I said, "Every day."

On Wednesday, March 4, the day of Father Hesburgh's funeral, U.S. Senators Joe Donnelly (D-IN) and Dan Coats (R-IN) and U.S. Representatives Mike Kelly (PA-03) and Jackie Walorski (IN-02) introduced concurrent resolutions in the Senate and House honoring the life of University of Notre Dame President Emeritus Fr. Theodore Hesburgh, C.S.C.

Donnelly said, "As a proud son of Notre Dame, I welcome the opportunity to honor Father Ted's incredible life. Father Ted worked with presidents, Popes, and Martin Luther King, Jr. on issues of nuclear nonproliferation, immigration reform, and civil rights.

"Yet it is his impact on the South Bend community, Notre Dame campus, and on those who attended Our Lady's University that I remember and celebrate. He wanted every single student, staff, and faculty member to know they were loved, cared about, and special. He taught us to live 'God, Country, Notre Dame.' May he rest in peace."

Coats said, "Father Hesburgh enriched innumerable lives with his visionary leadership and faithful service. He was a powerful voice on numerous important issues, including civil rights, higher education and faith. It was a pleasure to know and learn from Father Hesburgh."

Kelly said, "Father Hesburgh lived an extraordinary life—one marked by devotion to God, dedication to country, and steadfast support for the community he loved so dearly. As president of the University of Notre Dame from 1952 to 1987, he transformed Catholic higher education in America and was a powerful moral voice in national affairs and the world.

"Over the course of his life, he faithfully served under four Popes and nine presidential administrations and received 150 honorary degrees, the most ever awarded to a single individual. Through it all, Fr. Hesburgh was a dedicated public servant grounded by deep faith, love for the poor, and a fundamental belief in the human rights of all people. This resolution will honor the life and memory of Fr. Hesburgh, and the great things he achieved for so many."

Walorski said, "Father Hesburgh's life epitomized what it means to serve this country. I hope every American takes a moment to learn his story and honor a truly inspiring man. He will be remembered for his convictions and revered for his contributions to higher education and to our entire country."

Honoring the life and memory of Reverend Theodore M. Hesburgh, C.S.C., president emeritus of the University of Notre Dame.
The Text of the Resolution Follows.

Whereas, Reverend Theodore M. Hesburgh, C.S.C., was born on May 25, 1917 in Syracuse, New York; ordained a priest of the Congregation of Holy Cross on June 24, 1943 in South Bend, IN; and served as president of the University of Notre Dame from 1952 to 1987;

Whereas, during his tenure, the University of Notre Dame welcomed women for the first time and embraced the spirit of open intellectual inquiry and moral engagement that defines it today;

Whereas, Father Hesburgh held a variety of appointed positions under four popes and nine presidential administrations;

Whereas, throughout decades of public service, Father Hesburgh proudly championed the civil rights of African Americans, our duty to the poor, and the fundamental human dignity of all persons;

Whereas, in pursuit of those ideals, Father Hesburgh held a variety of influential public roles, including terms as a founding member and chairman of the U.S. Commission on Civil Rights, chair of the Overseas Development Council, chair of the Select Commission on Immigration and Refugee Policy, and as the permanent representative of the Holy See to the International Atomic Energy Agency in Vienna from 1956 to 1970;

Whereas, in pursuit of global social justice, Father Hesburgh reaffirmed the University of Notre Dame's commitment to human rights by helping to found the Kellogg Institute for International Studies and the Kroc Institute for International Peace Studies at the University as well as the Center for Civil and Human Rights at the University of Notre Dame Law School;

Whereas Father Hesburgh was a longtime advocate for the responsible stewardship of atomic energy and gracefully brought together scientists, scholars, and spiritual leaders to work toward an end to nuclear conflict;

Whereas, Father Hesburgh served as ambassador to the 1979 United Nations Conference on Science and Technology for Development, the first Catholic priest to formally hold a diplomatic position for the United States Government;

Whereas, Father Hesburgh received both the Congressional Gold Medal and the Presidential Medal of Freedom, the nation's highest civilian awards, as well as more than 150 honorary degrees, the most ever awarded to a single individual;

Whereas, Father Hesburgh passed away on Thursday, February 26, 2015 but remains very much alive in the hearts of all who knew him and the University that he loved: Now, therefore, be it.

During the public memorial service of March 4, 2015 at the Purcell Pavilion, President Barack Obama sent a video message. Here is the text of that message.

"Good evening, everyone. I'm sorry I couldn't be with you tonight to remember a friend and celebrate a remarkable life on this earth.

"As you know, Father Ted Hesburgh filled many roles throughout his life: spiritual leader, allies of popes and presidents, even representative to the International Atomic Energy Commission. But beyond any other title, the one he cherished most was Father Ted, humble servant of God.

"Father Ted took the helm at Notre Dame during a time of great change for the Church and for the nation. A steady hand guided by his fundamental decency helped to turn this University into a world-renowned center of higher learning, a place where faith and reason, clergy and laity could all come together and flourish.

"Fifty years ago this week, as Catholic priests and nuns traveled to join brave marchers in Selma, Father Ted was one of the six leaders serving on our nation's Civil Rights Commission.

"There's a story that I love from the early years of that commission, back when Father Ted was a founding member. As you can imagine, those discussions were often long and difficult because, as he later wrote, the commission agreed on very little outside of the Constitution. So when it came time to write their final report, Father Ted had an idea. He took them all to the Notre Dame retreat up in Land O'Lakes, Wisconsin.

"There he said they realized that despite their differences, they were all fishermen in the literal sense. So they fired up the grill, caught some walleye and ultimately the report they produced served as a major influence on the Civil Rights Act of 1964. That's the spirit that we celebrate today. A leader, a thinker, a man who always saw that we are all children of God and that together we can do incredible things that we can't do alone.

"I was so honored to meet Father Ted and encouraged graduates to follow his example when I delivered the commencement address of Notre Dame almost six years ago. It's an example worth following in our own lives, as we reflect on his.

"Rest in peace, Father Ted. May God bless you all and may God bless the United States of America.

CHAPTER 2
A DISCIPLE OF FATHER HESBURGH

In 1996, I saw Father Hesburgh at a function at Notre Dame. We had talked a few years earlier, just after I left the White House where I had worked for President George H.W. Bush (1992-93). During that two-hour visit, we spoke about subjects that ranged from world hunger to civil rights to the future of college athletics.

At this function in 1996, he asked me, "So, what have you been doing?" I told him I had been working for ESPN and I had started a mentoring program in South Bend public schools. He looked at me and said, "No, what have you really been doing?"

I had heard the story of Jose Napoleon Duarte, a member of the Notre Dame Class of 1948 who had taken a course in social justice under Father Hesburgh when he was a student. He came to Notre Dame by train through Central America with his brother from El Salvador. In fact, when Duarte was a freshman, one of his first classes was on social justice with Father Hesburgh. He was in his first year as a Notre Dame professor.

"I nearly threw him out of class the first day," Father Ted said. "He was speaking Spanish to his brother during class." But Hesburgh found out that "Nappy" as he called him, could not speak much English and was having trouble understanding Father Ted. His brother was merely trying to interpret what he did not understand.

Fluent in Spanish, Hesburgh offered to meet with Duarte after class and give him lessons in English. That led to a strong bond between pupil and teacher, one that lasted 46 years.

Duarte returned to El Salvador, where he was employed as an engineer. But his homeland was in a chaotic state in terms of the political climate.

In 1960 on a trip to Panama City for a Universal Notre Dame Night, Hesburgh and Duarte met. Hesburgh looked at him and asked, "Nappy, what are you doing?" Duarte told him he was a civil engineer in El Salvador. "It's time for you to take your country and lead it out of that dictatorship and communism, and bring in democracy," Father Hesburgh told him.

It was not an easy path to becoming the only Notre Dame graduate to serve as president of a country. Duarte founded the Christian Democratic Party and ran for President in 1972. It was a revolution that was well received by many. He was winning handily when the army stopped the count and declared its candidate the winner.

A few weeks later, Duarte supported a dissident military faction and it failed. Duarte was arrested, beaten and told he would be shot. After help from Hesburgh and others from the United States, he was allowed to leave the country and spent the next seven years in Venezuela.

A different regime came into power in 1979 and Duarte was allowed to return to his homeland. He was elected President in 1984 and served in that capacity until 1989. He was the first civilian to serve as president of El Salvador in half a century.

In 1985 Duarte came to Notre Dame to receive an honorary degree from Notre Dame at the May commencement. During his speech, he said he hoped to return home to El Salvador in the style of Notre Dame football legend George Gipp and score a victory for peace. There had been five years of civil war in his country.

"George is up there, with all the distinguished saints we have in heaven, and through him I want to invoke the help and protection of God," said Duarte, who actually had a one day tryout with the Notre Dame team when he came to school.

Duarte died on Feb. 23, 1990 (just three days from the day on the calendar that Hesburgh died 25 years later). He was just 64.

When he died, President George H.W. Bush said, "He was the father of Salvadoran democracy. He exhibited courage in building the foundation of democracy in El Salvador and the message of hope he brought to all of Central America."

Hesburgh was greatly saddened at the passing of one of his first and more remarkable students. "He was a man who was honest in a situation where very few are all that honest," Hesburgh was quoted as saying. "He gave all he had to bring out social justice in a country that was characterized by a culture of violence."

So when Hesburgh asked me, "No, what are you really doing?" I thought of Duarte immediately.

I had a visit with Fr. Ted when I returned from the White House in 1993. We had discussed the educational crisis in this country and we talked about what it would take to improve the secondary school system. I told him how the schools not only needed better teachers, but the basic physical environment needed time, work and money. I could see that in the schools in South Bend.

My discussion with Father Ted sparked an idea to improve the infrastructure of the schools in South Bend. I thought if I could establish a blueprint for success here, other cities across the country could adopt it, and we would have an impact nationally.

Jimmy Carter's Habitat for Humanity, which builds homes for the poor, gave me some ideas, as did the Christmas in April project, which involved hundreds of Notre Dame students who fix neighborhoods in South Bend during the spring.

In early 1997, I spoke to a Rotary Club luncheon in South Bend and challenged them to fix up the local schools and expand the after-school programs. The after-school programs were just as important because most of the juvenile crimes are committed between 3 p.m. and 5 p.m. during the week.

Over time the corporate sector became involved. I got Sherwin Williams of Ohio to donate $20,000 worth of paint and brushes. I told local corporations in South Bend I was putting down $5,000 of my own money and challenged them to match it. We had an initial goal of $175,000, but reached $200,000 by the end of the project.

The media got involved—the news and the sports side. I had met Anne Thompson, a Notre Dame grad at NBC news, and she contacted the Today Show about the program. Jack Ford, who is today still one of the most respected sports journalists in the country, interviewed me on the morning of June 20, 1998.

That was quite a day. Over 700 volunteers showed up to revitalize Lincoln Grammar School in South Bend. When I saw those busloads of volunteers pull in, it gave me a great feeling. We accomplished a lot, and worked through the summer on the project.

There were a couple of articles in the local

papers about the project and I sent them to Father Hesburgh, and to former president George H.W. Bush, a friend for 45 years. I still value their correspondence, which I have kept all these years.

Dear Digger,

Thanks ever so much for sending me that interesting information about Lincoln School and all that you are doing as a true "Point of Light." I am so glad that you are still involved in helping students — but who's surprised?

Warmest regards, old friend. I miss our visits from the past.
Sincerely,
George

Dear Digger,

I finally had a few free moments tonight to read all those wonderful articles you sent to me. I am very proud of what you are doing. I wish you all success in this endeavor, which could turn around the disastrous situation in most of our schools, especially in poor neighborhoods.

I hope it is helpful to know that both Father Ned and I are very proud of what you are doing and cheering loudly from the sidelines. The community needs leadership like this and you are really giving it. I know the effect will be outstanding.
Keep up the good work.

Ever devotedly in Notre Dame,
Rev. Theodore M. Hesburgh, C. S. C.
President Emeritus, University of Notre Dame

It was one of the most rewarding projects of my career. And, Father Ted Hesburgh inspired it all.

New Orleans

In 2007, after Hurricane Katrina hit New Orleans, I worked through the Rotary to build two homes for families in New Orleans, then worked to restore John McDonough High School. New Orleans had always been one of my favorite cities back to when I first recruited the area in 1973.

In 2007, then in 2009, we finished those homes and the day we gave the keys to those families brought me to tears.

McDonough High School was in bad shape and it was my intention to get corporations to help in the restoration. We went on the MSNBC program "Morning Joe" and talked about the school.

The school's basketball court had warped wood and the auditorium had a leaky ceiling. I challenged Robbins Sports Surfaces, the company that built the basketball courts for the Los Angeles Lakers and University of North Carolina, to build John McDonough High a new basketball court.

Ten minutes after the show, a guy showed up with a pad and a tape measurer. Security came to me and said, 'This guy has come to see you about the floor.' His name was Joe Covington from Covington Floors out of Birmingham, Alabama; he installs Robbins Sports courts."

Covington was in New Orleans for a meeting when he received a call about the challenge I made to Robbins Sports Surfaces. The call was from Jay Stoehr, the company's president, who told Covington that Robbins Sports Surfaces needed to put in the court at John McDonough High after the on-air challenge.

Robbins Sports Surfaces announced they would install the court and soon after Starbucks donated $125,000 to fix the ceiling in the auditorium.

"Go Visit Father Ted"

I still speak in dorms and to various groups at Notre Dame throughout the year. I used to speak at freshman orientation when it was run by the legendary Emil T. Hoffman, who just died a couple of years ago. What Father Hesburgh was to Notre Dame, Emil T. was to the Freshman Year of Studies.

I don't know if I made a difference in those kids lives, but I thought it was necessary to speak about the mystiques and traditions of the school, the traditions that made Notre Dame special in athletics and outside of athletics.

I always finished my presentation talking about the power of a Notre Dame degree. "Once you graduate you will see the Notre Dame network shows up. All over the country there are people from Notre Dame in all lines of business and they are there to help. Notre Dame people get involved and the deal will be closed.

"That is what is so important about the impact this place has on your life. You don't see it until you leave. If you are here four years, you will get it. When you graduate you become one of those people who makes a difference in other peoples lives."

Prior to Father Ted's death, whenever I spoke in the dorms or to the MBA students, or at freshman orientation I made sure to tell them to go see Father Ted and get a blessing. "He is up there in the 13th floor of the library, take advantage of the opportunity."

I made a point of it especially with the MBA students. Each year the new class of MBA students had about 60 in it, but only about 10 were Notre Dame grads. I would tell those undergrads from other schools, even the ones from (football rival) Southern Cal, all about Father Hesburgh and what he had done, not only for Notre Dame, but for this country.

"You need to go visit Father Hesburgh. The

torch is being passed to you. You made a choice to come here and you need to carry on the torch with you when you leave." Meaning, serve your fellow man.

The biggest examples of that are seen in the Notre Dame clubs all over the world. No one has a network of alumni clubs like Notre Dame. Sure, they are active at football and basketball games when the Irish teams go on the road. But, they are just as active when it comes to community service projects in their hometown.

Our Program is Bigger than Basketball

Throughout my Notre Dame career I always felt it was important to provide my players with an education that was more than just basketball. It was basically an approach where "Our Program is bigger than basketball."

Sure, it was important that they graduate. All 56 of my players received their degrees from Notre Dame. There were many things we did to give them a total education. My job was to get them from playing basketball to playing the game of life.

When I coached we used to travel commercially, not charters like most of the teams take today. With such a national schedule, we went all over the country and I tried to work in some educational experiences, when we had the time. This was especially the case when we played multiple games on the same road trip during the semester break.

For instance, when we played at Maryland we worked in a tour of the White House or other sites in Washington, D.C. It took some extra planning and advance work, but it was worthwhile and I think my former players would agree today that it was educational and added to the camaraderie of the team.

I always put the front page of the Chicago Tribune on the wall in the locker room. Then before a practice I asked someone on the team about something that was on that front page. It could be something that was national headlines or of interest locally.

One day I asked the team about what was on the front page of the Chicago Tribune. One of the freshmen raised his hand and said, "Congress is meeting in Washington, D.C. this week." He said it like Congress is a traveling road show that meets at different areas around the country. I explained to him that Congress always meets in Washington, D.C.

We had team Mass the day of each game and I had the players and the managers do the readings. We started the season with the seniors and worked our way to the freshmen. I was not trying to force Catholicism down anyone's throat. But doing the readings was a way to get the guys experience in public speaking.

It was all part of the preparation for life after basketball. They were going on a job interview at some point and were going to have to communicate. I made sure all of my seniors had interviews scheduled during their senior year.

You read many stories today about athletic teams that perform various community service activities throughout the country. We were one of the first programs that was actively involved in these projects. Dating back to my first year at Notre Dame (1971-72), we became involved with Logan Center, a facility for people with special needs.

Our involvement was because of Hesburgh. Notre Dame has had a strong tradition of community service, it is a basic mission of the school, one that Hesburgh pushed from day one when he became president in 1952. Today over 80 percent of Notre Dame students are involved in some kind of community service in South Bend or in their hometown. Father Ted is smiling from heaven.

Logan Center

Stan Peziak was a friend who ran the Linebacker Bar in South Bend. In his spare time Stan used to volunteer at the Logan Center.

Just before Christmas my first year he asked me if I could get some coaches together from Notre Dame and play the Special Olympics

Team from Logan Center in a basketball game.

One of the Special Olympians was Butch Waxman, a 24-year-old at the time who loved basketball, and we hit it off from the outset. The gym at Logan Center was packed with the disabled kids from the center. Before the game, I got my team together and told them how we were going to play this game.

"At the end, we will be up two points," I said. "Let Butch score, then I'll let him steal the ball from me and score again to put them up by two. Then I'll take a last shot and miss and they will win by two."

The plan went according to script and the place went crazy. After the game we had a Christmas party and dinner and Santa even showed up to give everyone gifts. I realized these people are God's little angels. I did some research and found that over six million people in this country are challenged in this way.

After the game I met Butch's parents, and they were terrific people. I asked them about Butch's life expectancy and they told me around 37 to 38 years old. I was very impressed with the people at Logan Center and the job they were doing, so I got more involved as the years went on. So did our players and it became one of the special areas of emphasis for community services activities for the entire Notre Dame community.

Who called timeout? We soon realized it was Butch!
(Photo by University of Notre Dame Sports Information)

Butch came to a lot of our games, and sometimes he came in the locker room before the game. In January of 1984-85, we played a Saturday game at Maryland and we stunk and lost by 12 points. It was our second loss in three games and we were starting to feel sorry for ourselves.

We had a quick turnaround and were playing Providence at home on Monday night. It was a game we had to win if we were going to make the NCAA Tournament.

About a half hour before the game, Butch and his friend Tommy came in the locker room. "You got beat by Maryland," said Butch. I said,

"We got killed by Maryland."

He continued to give me a hard time about that game. I finally told him, "You want to talk to the team? They will be back in here in a couple of minutes."

When the team came back in, much to the shock of my assistant coaches, I let Butch and Tommy give the pregame talk.

Providence's game plan was on the board, so Tommy and Butch started reviewing it. They pointed to Tim Kempton and called him Ken Barlow, and pointed to Jim Dolan and called him Tim Kempton. But the guys nodded their heads like they were following along. Finally I said, "OK guys, let's go." If my team was feeling sorry for itself earlier in the day, they weren't now.

At halftime I was sitting on the bench looking at the stat sheet and Butch was sitting next to me. He always sat in the stands during the game with a social worker named Dave from Logan Center, but as time was winding down on the halftime clock, Dave was nowhere to be seen.

The horn sounded and still no Dave. I told Butch to take my seat on the bench. I didn't know what else to do. Butch was now sitting among my assistant coaches. They really thought I had lost it now.

The second half started and about three minutes in someone from our bench shouted,

"Time out!" I looked at my assistants and they were all startled.

It was Butch; he wanted a timeout. Fortunately, none of the officials heard it. "Butch, what are you doing?," I asked him.

"I want to talk to the team," was his reply. I then went to the end of the bench and grabbed one of my managers. "Go find Dave. Now!" We went on to win the game, 70-63. Tommy and Butch came into the locker room and high-fived all the players and coaches as if they had won the game.

After that first game against Butch in 1971, I told the people at Logan Center I would play in the Christmas game as long as Butch played. Every year it was played the Sunday before Christmas and I even worked our schedule around it. Two seasons I actually moved Notre Dame games to accommodate the Logan Center game, once for a road game at Valparaiso and once for a home game against UCLA.

We played in 30 consecutive Christmas games against the Logan Center Olympic team and Butch hit the game winner over me all 30 years. Butch passed away in August of 2010. He lived to be 63.

Motivating My Former Players

I still remember the first time I saw Monty Williams play. We were at an AAU tournament in Los Angeles during the summer and I was watching his D.C. All-Star team. Monty was a kid no one had heard much about, but he was dominating the game. I called over to Pete Gillen, who had been one of my assistants and was now the head coach at Xavier. I said, "Peter come watch this kid Williams. But don't get any ideas, he's mine."

When I got back to South Bend I checked his grades. He was near a 4.0 student, and in fact he made a 4.0 his senior year. At the time he was the all-time sleeper. We brought him out for a visit and he committed right away. Then his senior year he averaged 30 points a game and scored 56 against DeMatha. With many major programs trying to recruit him, Monty stayed true to his commitment.

He had a terrific freshman year in 1989-90, my last NCAA Tournament team. He started 18 games and averaged almost eight points a game. At 6-7 he could do just about everything. I could see that we were going to build our team around him down the road.

On September 4, 1990, just five weeks before practice, Monte had a routine physical with the rest of the team. During the physical our doctors discovered a problem with his heart. He was diagnosed with HCM (Hypertrophic Cardiomyopathy), a rare but potentially dangerous condition featuring a thickened muscle between chambers of the heart.

Hank Gathers of Loyola Marymount had just died of a heart problem the previous March.

It was different from Monty's problem, but awareness was high. So, on September 28, 1990, after he had gone through many more tests, we announced Monty Williams was through with basketball. It was tough for Monty to accept because he didn't have any abnormal symptoms.

That year, I tried to involve Monty in the team as much as possible. At the beginning of the season I asked him to put his uniform on and to appear in the team photo. When all the players were dressed and ready to go, he was still back in the locker room. He couldn't bring himself to do it, so he put his jeans and shirt back on and left the building. He sat on the bench for most of the games and we took him on trips. But it was difficult.

After I left, he didn't want anything to do with the team. In fact, on nights Notre Dame played at home, he used to go to the Rockne Memorial and play pickup games. Sometimes he was all by himself just shooting jumpers pretending he was making moves against Grant Hill or Jalen Rose.

He sat out two years. Prior to the 1992-93 season, the Notre Dame physicians heard about the case of Steve Larkin, Barry's brother (and the brother of 1984 Notre Dame football captain Mike Larkin), who had the same problem as Monty. Steve had been cleared to play after having a test run at the National Institute of Health in Bethesda, Maryland, ironically just a few miles from Monty's hometown in Forest Heights, Maryland.

Monty had the test and the doctors determined he could play. It was quite a test.

They basically shocked his heart, trying to give him a heart attack. There were 12 doctors in the room when they gave it to him. But he came through it just fine. He played the 1992-93 and 1993-94 seasons for John McLeod, averaging over 20 points a game for a 56-game period.

I always held my breath when I saw him play, but I was thrilled he was able to return to the court. He went on to play in the NBA through 2002-03, the last of my 22 former players to play in the NBA.

Today he is one of the most respected coaches in basketball. He was the head coach of the New Orleans Pelicans for five years and was an assistant coach under Mike Krzyzewski with the United States Olympic team. He is now the Director of Basketball Operations for the San Antonio Spurs.

We saw the true Monty Williams in 2015 when he had to deal with the death of his wife, the result of a freak automobile accident in

Oklahoma. His eulogy for his wife went viral on the internet. I can't remember when I was more proud of one of my former players.

I spoke with Monty after the funeral and later in the summer. I was just sick for him, but so proud of him at the same time. It made me feel good about the way we had prepared him for life after basketball.

In many ways, it all went back to Father Hesburgh.

CHAPTER 3
HESBURGH'S STARTING FIVE

Hesburgh's Last Suppers

I had always been close with Father Hesburgh, but I spent more time with him socially in his later years. Six or seven times a year we would go to our favorite Italian restaurant in South Bend, Parisi's. It is located on South Bend Avenue. It is a popular place all year, but especially on Notre Dame home football weekends. At one time you could see it from the edge of the Notre Dame campus, but the new Eddy Commons Street district now blocks the view from the stadium and Joyce Athletic Center.

Father Hesburgh had a private network of friends that included myself, my fiancé Linda, his officer assistant Melanie Chapleau, Roberto Parisi, the owner of the restaurant, Father Austin Collins and Father Paul Doyle. Our waitress was Diana Stabnik, Roberto's life companion.

One of the reasons we went to Parisi's was because Father Hesburgh loved Alfredo sauce. When he was Notre Dame President and traveled to the Vatican he became friends with Cardinal Giovanni Montini of Milan. Cardinal Montini used to take him to Alfredo's restaurant in Rome where they invented Alfredo sauce.

It just so happened that Cardinal Montini became Pope Paul VI.

So the group of us would take Father Ted to Parisi's and Roberto would make his best

Alfredo sauce for his pasta. He loved it. Father Ted would also order a Manhattan now and then, but we made sure to have the bartender make it 80 percent iced tea.

He also loved to smoke a good cigar. I would get him some good Cuban cigars through some friends of mine. I told him which ones were Cuban and which ones were Dominican because the Cubans went in the left pocket and the Dominicans were in the right pocket so he wouldn't get them confused.

Parisi's was a place where Hesburgh could relax among friends. Invariably, he was the center of attention and conversation. I remember talking to him about his brother, Jim Hesburgh, who was 20 years younger and a successful business man. "Why did you become a priest," I asked. "I was born to be a priest," he replied simply.

Often we had conversations about current events, but there were also nights that Father Ted talked about his personal history with the Civil Rights Commission.

One night I asked him to pick his "starting five."

"In your life with all these people you have met around the world, give me your starting five."

He looked at me with a smile and said, "You are still coaching."

December 9, 2014, our last dinner at Parisi's. Our group included Father Paul Doyle, Roberto Parisi, Diane Stabnik, Digger Phelps, Father Austin Collins, Linda Costas, Father Ted Hesburgh, Melanie Chapleau.

Here are the people he picked that night:

Pope Paul VI

Pope Paul VI was the first person he mentioned. As I said above, they met when Father Ted went to Rome on business at the Vatican. In addition to their dinners at Alfredo's restaurant in Italy, they spent many hours discussing theology, philosophy, world hunger…in general, the problems of the world.

On one trip after he became Pope Paul VI, he invited Hesburgh to his office in the Vatican and asked him to become a Cardinal. It was The Pope, Father Ted and the Pope's secretary sitting in the Pope's office.

Pope Paul VI said, "This Ring is yours," as he pointed to a Cardinal's ring on the desk.

Father Ted took the ring, put it in his pocket and said, "No, I am a priest." They talked it over for an hour, but Father Hesburgh stuck to his guns and continued to respond, "I am a priest."

Father Hesburgh left the office and the Pope's secretary at the time grabbed him by the arm and said, "You stupid Americano." He could not believe Father Hesburgh was turning down the Pope.

Father Ted went back to see the Pope years later. The secretary asked Father Ted, "Where's the ring?"

"In my office at Notre Dame," said Father Ted. When he died, that ring was still in his office.

Father Ted told me another reason why he didn't accept the Cardinal appointment was he didn't want anyone in Rome to tell him how to run Notre Dame.

President Dwight D. Eisenhower

The second person Hesburgh mentioned for his starting five was President Dwight D. Eisenhower. They had a close relationship that began when Eisenhower was president. Ike respected what Father Ted was doing at Notre Dame and he was the first president to see

Two of Hesburgh's starting five came to the 1960 Notre Dame graduation. President Dwight D. Eisenhower was the commencement speaker and Pope Paul VI said the graduation Mass.

Father Hesburgh as a leader who could have an impact on the world stage.

Ike was the President who first appointed Father Ted to a national commission. In 1954, he appointed him to the National Science Board.

Of course the most important presidential appointment Father Ted had was also offered by Eisenhower. In 1957 he asked him to be a part of the new Civil Rights Commission. He served on that commission for 15 years, including the final three years as Chairman.

I will get into this in more detail in chapter 5, but Eisenhower was quite frankly surprised by what the Commission accomplished and he knew Father Hesburgh was a big reason. The six-man committee had three from the North and three from the South, three Democrats, two Republicans and one independent (Hesburgh).

Thanks to Father Ted moving a key final meeting to the Notre Dame retreat house in Wisconsin the group agreed on 12 basic principals, 11 unanimously.

At the White House meeting to review the principles, Ike turned to Father Ted and asked how the group was able to agree upon so much.

Father Ted said he did not appoint three men from the South and three from the North, or men from different parties, he had appointed six fishermen. All six had fished that day before their night meeting.

Father Edmund P. Joyce, C.S.C.

The third person Father Hesburgh mentioned in his starting five that night at Parisi's was Father Edmund P. Joyce. That was no surprise because he and Father Ted worked hand-in-hand for 35 years.

Father Joyce was Father Ted's executive vice president from day one when he became president in 1952. Joyce was the person in charge of the university when Father Ted was away between 1952-70. Then Notre Dame hired a Provost who was officially in charge in Father

Ted's absence, but you can believe if a decision had to be made the first person the Provost called was Father Joyce.

And Father Joyce was always the first person Father Ted talked with in consultation before making any major decision involving the university, especially when it came to athletics.

It would be impossible to recount, all the great things he did for Notre Dame.

Father Hesburgh was once quoted as saying, "Without him (Father Joyce), both the university and I would not have been as successful. When I went away from campus for long periods of time I never gave it a second thought. He knew exactly what needed to be done.

"In a very real sense, Ned was the anchor of the executive echelon during those years.

"Many vice presidents came and went, but Ned was always there. …He was, and is, a man of impeccable moral character, shrewd judgment, rocklike fidelity, and unfailing dependability."

Joyce and Hesburgh first met the day Joyce was ordained a priest (June 8, 1949). The ceremony took place in the Sacred Heart Basilica. Hesburgh, who was the executive vice president under Father John Cavanaugh at the time, ran into Joyce after the ceremony outside of his office.

I went to Father Joyce's funeral in 2004 and

Father Hesburgh gave a detailed account of their first meeting in his eulogy:

"My door burst open and out came this handsome, ebullient young priest with a Holy Cross habit on. I said, 'You've got to be Ned Joyce.' Father Joyce responded, 'Yes, who are you?'

"I introduced myself and knelt down and said, 'You'd better give me that first blessing. It's one of the best.'"

So Hesburgh was the first person that Joyce blessed on the day he became a priest.

It didn't take Joyce long to impress Hesburgh, who was on a fast track to the Notre Dame presidency in 1949. Joyce did not go into the seminary after graduating from Notre Dame in 1937. The first person from the state of South Carolina to attend Notre Dame (as a freshman in 1933), Joyce returned to his home in Spartanburg, passed the CPA Exam and became an accountant.

After five years in that profession, Joyce had a calling and returned to Notre Dame and entered the seminary. At first he was an assistant rector in Morrissey Hall and taught theology. However, after just one semester, Father John Burke, the financial vice president at the time, became sick with nephritis and had to go to Arizona to recover.

Father John Cavanaugh, then Notre Dame

President, was aware of Joyce's experience in the business world, and put him in charge of the school's finances on a temporary basis. Joyce did a great job. When Burke returned, Joyce went to Oxford to pursue a degree in philosophy, political science and economics.

Father Ted had already felt Joyce would be a significant player on his team when he became president and he enthusiastically endorsed Cavanaugh's recommendation that Joyce go to Oxford to be exposed to academic areas he probably had not studied previously when he was an accountant.

After a year at Oxford, where Joyce played on a world championship basketball team, Cavanaugh brought him back to replace Father Burke full time. Burke soon passed away as a result of the nephritis.

A year later, Father Cavanaugh appointed Hesburgh as university president and sure enough he picked Father Joyce to be his executive vice president.

When you look at it, this Hesburgh-Joyce team worked efficiently together because they were so opposite. Father Joyce was from South Carolina and Father Hesburgh from Syracuse, NY. Father Joyce was a good athlete and Father Hesburgh used to tell us he had two left feet.

I wouldn't call Father Hesburgh a liberal, but he was much more liberal than the very conservative Father Joyce. Father Joyce took time with decisions and Father Hesburgh was much more impulsive, and more of a risk taker.

In 1972, after women were allowed to enroll at Notre Dame, Hesburgh went to Joyce with the idea that they should switch jobs. But, Father Joyce said, "We are fine, let's continue the way things are. " So they worked together for another 15 years in the same roles.

Joyce was in charge of the books and the athletic department for 35 years and he was terrific to work with. He was very supportive of our program from day one.

I feel Father Joyce liked the way I ran our basketball program. We never had an NCAA investigation, never had a player arrested, and I followed my budget closely. And, we averaged almost 20 wins a year.

I gained a lot of credibility with him in 1979. I scheduled a game with Michigan and my good friend Johnny Orr for the Pontiac Silverdome outside of Detroit for the 1978-79 regular season finale. I thought this would be a national game of interest as we had gone to the Final Four the previous year and Michigan had been to the National Championship game three years previously. In fact, Johnny and I thought we could break the NCAA attendance record, which then was 52,693 for the UCLA vs. Houston game in the Astrodome in 1968.

We didn't get the record, but 37,000 fans showed up. Each school took home $108,000 from that game, just $8,000 less than what each team got from the NCAA for going to the Final Four that year.

One day Athletic Director Moose Krause came into Father Joyce's office with that check for $108,000. Father Joyce, said, "Where did this come from?" Moose said, " It is from that Michigan game Digger scheduled."

That certainly made Father Joyce's day because that money was not in the original budget for the basketball program that year. We did the same thing in the Super Dome with LSU 11 years later.

When Father Joyce passed away, there were people from all over the country and all walks of life at the funeral service. Father Joyce did not get the attention Father Hesburgh received as he preferred to stay behind the scenes. But his respect level, especially within the athletic community, was significant.

Father Hesburgh said at the funeral that they had an agreement that whoever went first, the other would give the eulogy. Father Ted also said he was going to follow an old Gregorian tradition and offer 30 masses in a row for the repose of Father Joyce's soul.

During that eulogy, Father Hesburgh read a letter from Major Pete Dawkins, the 1958

Heisman Award winner, who worked with Father Joyce on many NCAA committees, and on the National Football Foundation board.

"Father Ned was always there when there was a problem," said Dawkins in the letter. "And, he always had an answer. But the thing that shone through him in that long series of relationships with the NCAA was that he believed athletes should be students and students should be athletes."

When Father Ned died in 2004, the NCAA was beginning to make significant reforms based on the recommendations that had been made by the Knight Commission. Hesburgh was co-chairman of that commission and many of the recommendations came from discussions between Hesburgh and Joyce. "Things are beginning to change (in college athletics) because of Ned," said Hesburgh at the funeral.

Near the end of his eulogy, Father Hesburgh simply said, "I've never known anyone in my life that was as wonderful a human being as Ned Joyce."

Helen Hosinski

As our discussion of Father Ted's Starting Five continued, I said, "You have to have a woman."

I said to myself before he gave me an answer, "it has to be Joan Kroc."

But, he gave me a different person, but one who meant so much to him and to his success as Notre Dame President. Helen Hosinski started working for Father Ted as his secretary when he became executive vice president under Father John Cavanaugh in 1949.

Helen ran the show in that office. She knew who to talk to, when and where he should go, what letters to read and what letters to throw into the garbage. You can imagine the correspondence Hesburgh received from all over the world.

In 1968, during the height of student unrest on campus, Father Ted wrote a famous letter telling students who interfered with the running of the university or the right of another student to go about his academic business, they had 15 minutes to meditate, then leave, or they would be dismissed.

Hesburgh got over 1,000 letters and there was a picture of Helen with the boxes of letters that circulated the country. I assume she typed a response from Father Ted to all of them.

All you need to know about how much Father Hesburgh respected Helen's work ethic is to look at the dedication in his autobiography, *God, Country, Notre Dame*. It is dedicated to Father Ted's mother, father, Father Joyce, and Helen Hosinski.

The most well known story about Helen

and Father Hesburgh took place in the spring of 1960. Father Ted had been rejected by a number of potential graduation speakers due to schedule conflicts and it was getting close to the June 5 graduation.

When another rejection came across Father Ted's desk, she asked, "Why don't you ask President Eisenhower? He is your good friend."

At this point in the modern era of Notre Dame, a President of the United States had never given a commencement address at Notre Dame.

While Hesburgh was always one to think outside the box and was a risk taker, he responded to Helen, "He is too busy, I am sure he can't come."

Helen pressed him on it. "Why don't you try?" Hesburgh responded with a smile, "Why don't you try."

She responded with vigor, "Okay, I will try to get President Eisenhower and you try to get one of your friends from Rome to come and say the Mass for the seniors."

So Helen, who in fact idolized Eisenhower for his war-hero accomplishments, wrote a letter of invitation and Father Hesburgh signed it. She had it delivered by special courier to the White House.

A few days later there was a response. With great joy, she told Father Ted that President

Eisenhower had accepted the invitation. She then asked, "Did you get one of your friends from Rome yet?"

Eisenhower accepted, even though Notre Dame's June 5 graduation was on the same weekend as his 45-year reunion at the US Military Academy. He left the reunion a day early so he could be at Notre Dame's Sunday graduation where he received an honorary degree, the first US President to be so honored by the University.

By the way, Hesburgh was successful in getting one of his friends to come from Rome for that Mass. Cardinal Giovanni Montini, who would become Pope Paul VI three years later, accepted Hesburgh's invitation.

That 1960 graduation started a tradition. Since then five other sitting US Presidents have been commencement speakers at Notre Dame's graduation, more than any other non-military institution. In addition to Eisenhower in 1960, Jimmy Carter (1977), Ronald Reagan (1981), George H.W. Bush (1992), George W. Bush (2001) and Barack Obama (2009) have also been to campus for graduation.

And the tradition started thanks to Helen Hosinski, one of Father Hesburgh's starting five.

Editor's Note:
We know Father Ted would also recognize the contributions that Melanie Chapleau made to his career after he retired from his post as president of Notre Dame. She worked for him as officer assistant for 28 years in his retirement. Father Ted's Starting Five took into account his time period as Notre Dame president.

Frank Leahy

The final member of Father Hesburgh's "Starting Five" really surprised me. I had always felt that there might have been a strained relationship between Father Hesburgh and Frank Leahy, the Notre Dame football coach from 1941-53 who won four National Championships, had four Heisman Trophy winners and won 87 percent of his games, still second to Knute Rockne in college football history. From 1946-49, the Irish did not lose a single game.

I said to Father Ted, "Leahy? You fired him!"

After four National Championships in the 1940s, Frank Leahy had become the face of Notre Dame and that was what the school was known for when Father Hesburgh took over as President in 1952. Shortly after he became president he was at a news conference on the West Coast and all the media in attendance were sports media. At the end of the press conference he was asked to assume the hiking position for a photo opportunity.

Father Ted had Father Joyce's job as executive vice president in control of the board on athletics from 1949-52. That meant he traveled with the football team on most of the trips and was the athletic department's liaison with the administration.

When Father Ted started in that position, he had a meeting with Father Cavanaugh. Cavanaugh told Hesburgh he was going to be vice president in charge of all the deans of the colleges. "They are out of control," said Cavanaugh. "And by the way, so is Coach Leahy. The kids are practicing football during class time. I want those kids in class, not practicing football."

So the first thing Father Ted did was get the Big 10 Conference manual and he read up on all the rules the Big 10 conference was using in regards to football and other sports. One of them was team travel. Big 10 teams took just 38 players on the road and Notre Dame was taking 44 or more. That seems like a very small number today, but in those days there was one-platoon football.

The second game of the 1949 season was at Washington. It was a three-day train ride from South Bend to Washington and the train left from Chicago on Wednesday. Hesburgh invoked the 38-player limit for that first trip and Leahy was not a happy coach. His original travel roster had 44 players on it and Father Hesburgh contacted him through Business Manager Herb Jones and asked him what six players he was taking off the travel roster. If he didn't then six players were going to be suspended from school for taking an unexcused absence.

Notre Dame, which had not lost a game since 1945, was trailing at halftime. It was a tense halftime locker room, but the Irish came back to win, 27-7. After the game, Leahy complained about the officiating and it received national attention.

The next week, Leahy was severely criticized in the media, and the social media of the day, hand written letters, were sent to Father Hesburgh by the box load for Leahy's crybaby attitude.

Father Ted called Leahy on the phone when they returned to campus. Realizing he had stepped over the line, Leahy apologized to Hesburgh.

"Are you getting a lot of mail Frank?"

"Two garbage containers full," said Leahy.

I said to Father Hesburgh as he told me the story, "What did you do with all the mail?"

Father Ted said, "I burned it."

Father Ted then told Leahy he wanted to meet with him. So they met and walked around the lakes on campus. Leahy thought he was in big trouble, especially after pouting about the numbers on the travel squad the previous week.

"Before I could start talking, Frank was apologizing," said Father Ted. "He knew all the articles were making Notre Dame look bad."

After Leahy had shown his remorse, Father Ted said, "Frank, I want you to know something. When I came back from the Washington game I had a meeting with (President) Father John Cavanaugh. From now on, any time we go west, you charter a plane. When we go to Southern California (in 1950), charter a plane."

Those players had missed five days of class, three going and two coming back and Father Hesburgh didn't want them missing so much class. So it was Hesburgh who started Notre Dame flying to games.

Bottom line, while they had their differences, Father Hesburgh had great respect for Frank Leahy and what he accomplished.

Hesburgh's First Presidential Appointment

"I really have no idea why President Eisenhower appointed me to the National Science Board," Hesburgh once said. "When the White House called and asked me, I asked them if they got the wrong Hesburgh.

"My whole background to that point was in philosophy and theology, not science. Of course I knew something about science from being president of Notre Dame with a college of science and college engineering.

"The person who called from the White House told me that President Eisenhower thought there ought to be a philosophical and theological point of view on the Science Board."

"So," Father Ted said, "that is fine then."

Father Ted always said that his time with the National Science Board was a great experience because he sat around a table with Nobel Prize winners who presented many points of view. "When you hear it (a scientific doctrine) from the guy who discovered it and got a Nobel Prize for it, that's a pretty good kind of education."

Father Hesburgh might have first earned Eisenhower's trust and respect early in Ike's presidency.

Father William Corby was a former Notre Dame President who is best known for giving general absolution to the Irish Brigade on the second day of the Battle of Gettysburg. He was the chaplain for the Irish Brigade. Every year since, a priest from Notre Dame will go back to

Gettysburg to say Mass on the anniversary of Father Corby's Mass.

In the early 1950s, shortly after Hesburgh took over as Notre Dame President and shortly after Eisenhower became President of the United States, Father Hesburgh went to Gettysburg to say the Mass.

Eisenhower had a farm in Gettysburg right next to the battlefield, where he went during his administration to reflect on difficult decisions and meet with world leaders. It was his Camp David.

Eisenhower learned that Father Ted was coming to Gettysburg and would be virtually in his backyard. Father Hesburgh invited President Eisenhower to come over for a visit and they met in a small room in Father Ted's hotel. Father Ted sat on the end of a bed and Eisenhower on a chair and they talked for an hour about the world's problems of the day.

CHAPTER 4
HESBURGH AND ATHLETICS

Hesburgh Sets the Tone

Just two years after he became Notre Dame's 15th president, Father Hesburgh was asked to write an article for Sports Illustrated. The September 27, 1954 issue was just the seventh for the weekly magazine and the article was written just before the opening of the football season, the first for 26-year-old Notre Dame Head Coach Terry Brennan, a former Notre Dame player who had taken courses taught by Hesburgh when he was an undergraduate.

While this article was written in just his second year as president, his basic theories of college athletics were no different compared to when I became head basketball coach 17 years later. As you can see he had an entertaining delivery and even made some points with a bit of levity, an underestimated quality of Hesburgh to those of us who knew him closely.

Below is a reprint of the first half of Hesburgh's article in that 1954 Sports Illustrated issue.

Almost everyone has something to say about intercollegiate athletics — especially during the fall of the year when experts are born as the multicolored leaves drift downward. I suppose that it is only fair to say that I am not an expert — not even an ex-athlete. My only excuse for having something to say is that I have listened to many of the experts, and have had dealings with a number of athletes.

All this was in the line of duty during a three-year stint as Chairman of our Faculty Board in Control of Athletics at the University. And it will be generally admitted that willy-nilly the President of Notre Dame must have a nodding acquaintance with the intercollegiate athletic world.

Broadly speaking, I have found two extreme attitudes in most of the experts. Those who favor intercollegiate athletics and praise it out of all proportion to its merits. And those who decry sports in college who are quite blind to the values that do exist on the playing field.

I realize that this amounts to saying that neither the friends nor the foes of intercollegiate athletics are quite honest, or let us say balanced, except against each other. However, whether you explain it by overenthusiasm or just plain ignorance, many of the experts seem to have missed the mark in assessing intercollegiate athletics.

One Spectator's Views

Now you can see why I take refuge in not being an expert. There is an old saying that the spectator gets the best view of the game. Here are a few things that one spectator has seen:

I should make it clear from the beginning that we are in favor of intercollegiate athletics at Notre Dame. Some would say: "And how!" Rather than leave it there, I must add that we favor intercollegiate athletics within their proper dimensions.

It goes without saying that the proper dimensions should be those of university life and purposes. But if this goes without saying, it does not happen without doing, and continual doing, on the part of those in charge of the university and athletics.

The fundamental difference between intercollegiate and professional athletics is that in college the players are supposed to be students first and foremost. This does not mean that they should all be Phi Beta Kappas or physics majors, but neither should they be subnormal students majoring in ping-pong.

Once this fundamental principle is accepted three equally obvious conclusions follow as the day the night.

First, any boy (Notre Dame was an all male institution in 1954) who has demonstrated during his high school days that he is quite incapable of doing collegiate work should not be admitted to college — even though he may have been an all-state high school fullback.

Secondly, once a qualified student who also happens to be a good athlete is admitted to college, he should follow the same academic courses, with the same academic requirements as the other students. Presumably he is in college for the same reason as the others: to get a good education for life, and to earn a degree in four years. This means, in practice, no fresh-air courses, no special academic arrangements for athletes.

Thirdly, the athlete should enjoy (and I use the word advisedly) the same student life in college as the other students. He should not be treated as prime beef, should not be given special housing and disciplinary arrangements, made a demigod on a special allowance who is above and beyond the regimen that is found to be educationally best for all the students of any given school.

In this connection, I am reminded of the animal who is enthroned and crowned with great ceremony at the annual Puck Fair in Ireland. It happens to be a goat.

As I read this piece, I had to smile because it was classic Hesburgh and they are familiar statements to me, principles that were presented when I interviewed to be Notre Dame's Head Basketball coach on April 30, 1971.

Earlier that week, Roger Valdiserri, the legendary sports information director, had given me a heads up that Notre Dame would be calling to interview, and that I had a good chance. Roger had a lot to do with me coming to Notre Dame.

We sat together at the Notre Dame at Marquette game in Milwaukee earlier that season, as I was there to scout the game for Fordham because we were playing Notre Dame and Marquette on consecutive Thursday nights in Madison Square Garden late in the season.

Roger followed our Fordham team closely after it was apparent Johnny Dee was going to retire at the end of the season.

Notre Dame thought about me more seriously when our Fordham team beat the Irish and All-American Austin Carr in Madison Square Garden 94-88 late that season in front of a sold out crowd of 19,500.

Getting back to April 30, 1971, I met Father Joyce at the airport in Detroit. Notre Dame always worked quickly when it came to replacing a football or basketball coach and this was an example. I was interviewing with Father Joyce before Roger had finished sending the Dee release out on the office telecopier.

The situation was just like 1941 when Father Frank Cavanaugh, brother of Notre Dame President John Cavanaugh, Father Hesburgh's predecessor, met Boston College Head Coach Frank Leahy in Albany, NY to interview him for the head football coach job.

At my interview with Father Joyce, many of the principles that Hesburgh talked about in that Sports Illustrated article were conveyed to me.

Father Joyce said, "We expect you to graduate your players, never get in trouble with the NCAA and be competitive." I asked him what he meant by competitive. He responded,

"About 18 wins a year." I had just won 26 games at Fordham, so surely I could win 18 games at Notre Dame.

Father Joyce also talked about Father Hesburgh's belief that student-athletes should be part of the student body. No athletic dorms, Mass the day of the game, a priest would travel with the team, and no transfers. And, most importantly, he expected the players to graduate, in four years.

These were all principles I supported whole-heartedly.

At the end of the interview, not that it mattered, we discussed the salary. He said $18,000 a year for four years, plus an additional $3,000 per year for radio and TV programs.

This was far below offers I was holding from Virginia Tech and Penn. Penn offered $35,000 a year.

But, this was my dream job. I would have taken the job for food coupons for my wife and kids at the South Dining Hall. In fact that four-year contract was the only multi-year contact I had in 20 years at Notre Dame. I worked from year to year after the 1974-75 season.

Hiring Ara Parseghian
From an athletic personnel standpoint, the most important hire that Father Hesburgh and Father Joyce made during their 35 years

together was bringing Ara Parseghian to campus. And, in many ways, it was for me also.

After the 1963 season, Notre Dame was in the middle of its worst football era. The program was 14-25 in the four-year period 1960-63, including two seasons with just two wins, and was on a stretch of five straight years without a winning season.

One of the schools that dominated Notre Dame during the stretch was Northwestern, and Head Coach Ara Parseghian. He was 4-0 against the Irish, including a 12-10 win at Notre Dame in 1961 when the Irish were ranked eighth in the nation entering the game.

Notre Dame was 23-3-2 against Northwestern before Ara became the Wildcats head coach and Notre Dame is 14-2 vs. the Wildcats since he left Evanston in 1964. Ara was 9-0 vs. Northwestern as Notre Dame coach after he had been 4-0 against the Irish. That might be the all-time example of "coaching does make a difference."

While Ara was a hot commodity at the time, this would be a hire outside the box for Hesburgh and Joyce. First, Ara was a Presbyterian, and Notre Dame had not hired a non-Catholic football coach since Knute Rockne in 1918. (Rockne converted to Catholicism in the middle of his career.)

Second, Ara was not a Notre Dame graduate.

Every Notre Dame coach had been a grad since Jesse Harper, who went to the University of Chicago and was Rockne's predecessor.

Third, Ara did not jump at the chance immediately, so there was a faction that wondered about considering someone who wouldn't jump at the chance after the first phone contact.

When I hear stories about his hiring process in December of 1963 it makes me think of the interview I had with Father Joyce at the Detroit airport in 1971.

Ara's interview took place at a hotel on the Southside of Chicago in December of 1963. Father Hesburgh told me they had to fight a blizzard to get there and the interview did not start until 9 p.m.

Right from the beginning, Father Ted wanted to make sure Ara was clear about the specific rules you had to follow to be the Notre Dame head coach under his watch.

"Ara have you read our articles of administration for athletics?" said Hesburgh. That was how Father Ted began. "Are you prepared to follow them to the letter? They are fairly strict.

"If you follow our rules to the letter and run this thing in complete honesty and follow the standards, which are very high, you will be OK. But if you get one inch off, then you are done."

How many University presidents have begun an interview with a prospective coach telling him what circumstances could come up that would lead to his dismissal?

But, Ara felt right at home with Father Ted and Father Ned from the beginning.

In a video about his decision to come to Notre Dame that was produced by the University of Notre Dame Athletic Department during the 125th anniversary of Notre Dame football, Ara said, "I felt very comfortable about it because I had coached at Miami of Ohio and Northwestern and my record was clean on that (NCAA rules) issue. It was a very positive point from both of our standpoints."

Of course, it proved to be one of the great hires in Notre Dame history. Parseghian put Notre Dame back in the National Championship conversation immediately. In his first year, 1964, Notre Dame was the talk of the country, winning its first nine games and reaching a No. 1 ranking. Only a last minute 20-17 loss at Southern Cal in the last game of the season prevented Notre Dame from winning the National Championship. John Huarte, who had not earned a letter until the 1964 season, won the Heisman Trophy.

In retrospect, this hire was important in my career, because Ara was my mentor when I came to Notre Dame. I had written him a letter in

1965 as a young high school coach and told him I wanted to coach at Notre Dame some day. Six years after writing that note, I was there with him.

I can't tell you how many times I went to him my first few years (Ara retired in 1974) for advice when it came to discipline, scheduling, or dealing with administration.

Ara won two National Championships (1966 and 1973) and never lost more than three games in a season. He finished with a 95-17-4 record in 11 seasons, a winning percentage of nearly 85. But most importantly, he had such a positive impact on so many young men who played for him, and on the Notre Dame community in general.

As I write this book, he is still going strong as he strives to find a cure for the Niemann-Pick disease that took the life of three of his grandchildren. He has to be considered one of the most respected people in the history of Notre Dame.

Ending the Bowl Game Ban
Notre Dame had a self-imposed football bowl ban between 1925 and 1968. That seems inconceivable today, but a look to the climate of college football and the determination of its national champion, and the academic schedule at Notre Dame shows where the ban came

from. It dated to 27 years before the start of Hesburgh's presidency when the Irish beat Stanford in the 1925 Rose Bowl, a contest that would be the final one for the Four Horsemen.

Going back to that 1954 Sports Illustrated article that Hesburgh penned, there is one principle that he did change over his career. Here is an excerpt:

Then, the critic adds, you have the temptation to commercialize athletics to pay the bills. To answer this, I return to my opening principle. There are no insurmountable temptations or dangers in intercollegiate athletics if the basic working principle is:

Always consider first the boy and his education. I will not deny the temptation to get the bills paid. For example, during the past 25 years, we have had the offer of a post-season bowl game almost every year, with a possible total income of millions of dollars.

We had four offers for postseason games last year (1953) alone. Notre Dame did play a bowl game in 1925. We will not play another. Why not? Because, as far as our students are concerned, we know that they cannot be engaged in as exciting a pursuit as football for three quarters of a semester and still maintain a 77 percent (academic) average.

If they do not have the required average, either they do not play the next year, or we lower our standards, and then they stop getting diplomas.

Like most temptations (if I might indulge in a little theology), this one involves a whole chain of further temptations. We don't want to start walking down that road. Because if we apply our basic principle of the boy's interest first, we cannot play one bowl game, and then a series of bowl games, despite the financial rewards involved.

The landscape of college football when it came to determining the national champion changed in 1968. Prior to 1968 the AP and UPI determined the national champion based on the regular season only. So, if Notre Dame didn't go to a bowl game, it was not a big deal. They could still win the National Championship.

Then in 1968 the AP changed and included bowl games in determining the national champion. The UPI held fast on its policy until 1974. That is why Notre Dame is listed as National Champion in 1973 by AP and Alabama is listed by UPI. Notre Dame won head to head in the Sugar Bowl, but UPI didn't have a post-bowl vote.

Another reason Hesburgh lifted the bowl ban in 1969, and the most important reason in his mind, is that Notre Dame changed its academic calendar. For the first time, the first semester ended before Christmas. There was no studying in between semesters and students could enjoy the holiday. And, the football team could prepare for a bowl game without concern for academics.

The end of the bowl ban was met with great joy by Notre Dame fans, who traveled to Dallas, Texas for the Cotton bowl of Jan. 1, 1970 in record numbers. Texas was ranked No. 1 in the nation and Notre Dame was eighth entering with an 8-1-1 record.

With the help of his assistant coaches, Parseghian mastered a defense to stop the Texas wishbone and he also had a few trick plays up his sleeve. One featured backup quarterback Jim Bulger completing a 37-yard pass to defensive back Clarence Ellis. It was the only offensive play of Ellis's career.

In the end, Texas prevailed 21-17 thanks to a touchdown pass from James Street to Cotton Speyer with just 1:08 left from, giving the Longhorns the National Championship. Notre Dame brought home $340,000 from that trip, a large sum nearly 50 years ago. Hesburgh took that money and put it to good use by adding it to the fund for minority student scholarships, a fitting decision for the man who was the Chairman of the Civil Rights Commission at the time.

The next year Notre Dame played Texas again in the Cotton Bowl and defeated the No. 1 ranked Longhorns 24-11 behind Joe Theismann, who was playing in his final game. Thanks to participating in the bowl game, the Irish improved to No. 2 in the final AP poll.

We Needed Hesburgh for This One

In late February of 1980 our basketball team was ranked in the top 10 according to UPI and DePaul was ranked No. 1 with a perfect 25-0 record. For the first time, the NCAA Tournament was going to seed teams and we were fighting to have as good a draw as possible. Obviously a win over the nation's top team would help that cause.

Ray Meyer, one of the most respected coaches in the nation and a member of the Notre Dame class of 1937, had taken DePaul to the Final Four the previous season and now had the Blue Demons undefeated. At 66-years-old he was getting better with age. Or at least he was getting better players and most of them came from right there in Chicago. His star player was Chicago native Mark Aguirre.

It was going to be a special night in the Joyce Center as it was Senior Night for Rich Branning and Bill Hanzlik, two of my best and most respected players in my 20 years as head coach. They were the model student-athletes in the Hesburgh athletic world.

With the challenge of playing No. 1, we needed to pull out all the stops. I needed to go straight to the top. Father Ted had said the pregame Mass for the San Francisco game three years earlier. The Dons, like DePaul another Catholic School, were 29-0 coming to South Bend and were ranked No. 1. We ended that streak and their No. 1 ranking, 93-82. San Francisco has not been No. 1 in basketball since.

We had a priest say Mass before every game and I usually told them, "Father, you've got 20 minutes and that includes the homily."

But I never said that to Father Hesburgh.

Father Ted had a great message for the Mass prior to the DePaul game. It made the players confident, but at the same time it put prayer in perspective. He talked about having the spirit and strength to do your best and playing to one's potential. When the players did that, they would win. He completed this homily by saying, "Special accomplishments do happen here, because it's Notre Dame."

This was a thrilling game, perhaps the best game in my Notre Dame career. It went double overtime with last second attempts by both teams at the end of regulation and the first overtime. With 39 seconds left and the score tied at 74, Orlando Woolridge was fouled. He had a one-and-one at the line and made both free throws to give us a 76-74 lead.

DePaul then took a timeout with 18 seconds left. They took a couple of shots in the final seconds, but they missed and we won, 76-74.

The students mobbed the court and our players cut down the nets, something we always did when we beat the No. 1 team.

In the immediate aftermath I went over to Father Ted. With my arm around him (see cover of this book), I said, "Father, a lot of prayers for this one." He said, "Digger, I was running out of Hail Marys."

Believe it or not, we never lost a game when Father Hesburgh said the pregame Mass and sat on the bench, a perfect 7-0. Three of those were wins over the No. 1 ranked team in the nation, San Francisco in 1977, Marquette in 1978 and DePaul in 1980.

Bill Laimbeer, 1975-79

The smartest frontcourt player I ever had also flunked out of Notre Dame. Fortunately, he came back... and graduated on time with his class.

Bill Laimbeer scored in the upper 10 percent on the SAT when he graduated from Palos Verdes High School in Los Angeles, Calif. But, when he came to Notre Dame he didn't think going to class was that important. He enjoyed going to the pool hall in the basement of the Student Union and the Notre Dame golf course at the edge of campus more than to class.

At the end his first semester and just days after he had a break out game off the bench at

UCLA, Laimbeer had a GPA between the 1.6 that would have allowed him to keep playing under NCAA rules, but not at the 2.0 needed to be eligible at Notre Dame.

We checked class attendance, but I was not of the opinion that we should go over to the dorm and walk him to class. He had to learn to be responsible, even if he flunked out.

It was a shame, because he was our third leading scorer and second leading rebounder at the time he became ineligible. He scored 15 points and had 14 rebounds against Manhattan in his last game that season (1975-76). Looking back, this was a team that had Adrian Dantley and other top players and could have gone to the Final Four.

With the games taken away from him we figured he would get his act together in the second semester and be ready to go for the 1976-77 season. We were wrong, as he did not cut it in the classroom in the spring either.

With two consecutive probation semesters, he was dismissed from school. But when he left he told me he wanted to come back to Notre Dame.

He transferred to Owens Technical School in Toledo, which was near his family's home. His dad was very successful in the business world, as he owned a corrugated box company. In fact, when Bill went to the NBA he was the only player in the league whose father made more money than he did.

I went to bat for Bill with Father Hesburgh.

Father Ted made the decision that he needed to get a 3.0 at Owens and then he would consider letting him return. Bill made the 3.0. Hesburgh then said he needed to come to summer school at Notre Dame and get two A's. Bill did that, and in August of 1977 he was readmitted.

That year we went to the Final Four for the only time in history, and his last year we went to the Regional Finals before we ran into Magic Johnson and Michigan State. He scored 509 points and had 433 rebounds in his 69 games at Notre Dame. I thought he could make it in the NBA as a center, but I never dreamed he would help lead Detroit to two World Championships.

That was a great example of how Hesburgh worked. He was going to make Bill work to get back into Notre Dame and make him realize the value of a Notre Dame education. It was a maturing process as much as an educational one for Bill and it is a reason he has been successful since he graduated as a player, a coach and in the business world.

Some Masses were for everyone, much to my chagrin

Father James Riehle was a Notre Dame

institution. He was the head of the monogram association for many years after I retired from coaching. But, for much of my career he was the team chaplain and held that position for multiple Notre Dame teams, so he made a lot of road trips with us, especially for big games. A lot of the male students at Notre Dame used to say that if they could have Father Riehle's job, they would join the priesthood.

I only got mad at Father Riehle one time. We were playing Michigan State and Magic Johnson for the right to go to the Final Four in 1979.

Somehow, the NCAA put us at a hotel that was flooded with Michigan State fans. Father Riehle was a friendly type and met some Catholic Michigan State fans in the lobby over the course of our stay.

The regional final was on a Sunday and we had Mass in one of the meeting rooms at the hotel. When we came in for mass Michigan State fans were everywhere. Some had brought pom-poms. I know a priest isn't supposed to keep people out of Mass, but it was not great mental preparation for our team. Playing Magic Johnson was going to be tough enough.

"Father, can't you say a second Mass for these Michigan State fans? Heck, have a collection and make some money."

Michigan State beat us 80-68 and went on to win the National Championship.

All Notre Dame athletic teams wore a tribute to Father Hesburgh after he passed away in February of 2015. (See right shoulder of Zach Auguste) The men's basketball team wore the tribute when it won its first ACC Championship just a month after Father Ted died.

Hesburgh Honored By Notre Dame Athletic Teams

When Father Ted passed away on February 26, 2015, the athletic department wanted to honor him by putting a Fr. Ted patch or sticker somewhere on the uniforms of all the teams. A patch was placed on the back of the helmets for the lacrosse teams and on the back of the helmets for the football teams.

At the first home event for sports that had a video board, a short film depicting Hesburgh's contributions to not only Notre Dame, but the world, was played.

The first home game the video was played for basketball, came on March 7, 2015 a game with Clemson. My co-author Tim Bourret, is the sports information director at Clemson and color commentator on the basketball games. He is a double domer and wanted to make sure the Clemson coaches and players knew what this video was all about since it was going to delay the start of the game a few minutes.

He also wanted the Clemson team to be respectful during that time. So he met with Clemson Coach Brad Brownell and told the players about Father Hesburgh. He told of his contributions through the Civil Rights Commission, something the African American players certainly related to.

Clemson players stood at attention through the entire pregame and looked up at the video attentively and with respect.

With that Fr. Ted patch on each player's jersey, Notre Dame made a great run to close the 2014-15 season, winning the ACC Tournament with victories in the state of North Carolina over Duke and North Carolina, and then reaching the Elite Eight of the NCAA Tournament.

Only a loss to an undefeated and No. 1 ranked Kentucky team by two points prevented a trip to the Final Four for the first time since our team in 1978.

Each Notre Dame team wore their respective

tribute to Hesburgh the following academic year as well. In 2015-16, the Notre Dame basketball team again went to the Elite Eight. This two-year run marked the first time Notre Dame had gone to the Elite Eight in consecutive years since we did it in 1977-78 and 1978-79.

No doubt, Father Hesburgh was looking down from Heaven on Mike Brey's program. The Irish were the only team in the nation to make the Elite Eight of the NCAA Tournament in both seasons.

CHAPTER 5
HESBURGH, THE GODFATHER OF CIVIL RIGHTS

As I said in chapter 3, our group loved to take Father Hesburgh to Parisi's restaurant in South Bend. We had many enjoyable dinners and these were times when he could just be himself and relax, and I'd pick his brain about his life experiences, many of which were landmark when it came to the history of our country.

I had an appreciation for civil rights at an early age. I was the son of an undertaker and at the age of 12 my dad taught me an important lesson. He would walk home from work because our funeral home was just a block away from our house in Beacon, NY. In fact, when we had "doubleheaders" (two funerals at nearly the same time), one of the bodies would be held in our living room.

One night at dinner with the entire family, my mom and my two sisters present, he said to us, "You kids have to understand that all religions are our religions, all cultures are our cultures and all colors of skin are our colors of skin."

That never left me.

We handled funerals for people from all races and religions and it just had a strong effect on me. My mother was quite an example also. She was a nurse, but with three kids, she never practiced the profession. She helped out considerably at the funeral home during the wake.

In those days the wake was two days and the

funeral was on the third day. She would nurse those families through the grieving period, and it was a tough time. I got involved also, even in the seventh and eighth grade. In high school I worked at night at the funeral home. Sometimes I had to go to the scene of a fatal accident, or go to the hospital and get the body and bring it to the morgue or to witness an autopsy.

That experience prepared me. It prepared me to treat all people the same.

Stamps for Thurgood Marshall and Malcolm X

I was on the Citizens Stamp Advisory Committee for 22 years and I will go into more detail about that in Chapter 9. I was one of nine people on that committee who determined what went on stamps.

Two of my proudest moments on the board took place when we approved stamps for two prominent African Americans. One was Judge Thurgood Marshall and the other was Malcolm X. I was passionate about both getting stamps and my connection to Father Hesburgh and his work in Civil Rights was a big reason.

Marshall was the first African American on the U.S. Supreme Court, an appointment he received from President Lyndon Johnson on June 13, 1967. He was a Supreme Court Judge for 24 years before retiring at age 82 for health reasons. He was replaced on the court by Clarence Thomas, another African American. In retirement, Marshall received the Franklin D. Roosevelt Freedom Medal and then posthumously received the Presidential Medal of Freedom from President Bill Clinton.

I was a Malcolm X fan, but the way I came to learn more about him was a bit unusual.

When I started work in the White House under President George H.W. Bush, there were two young men, Orlando and J.J., working at the Hyatt Regency in Bethesda where I was staying at the time. They were good guys but they were street guys. They knew who I was from my time as coach of Notre Dame basketball, but they told me they wouldn't trust me until I read *The Autobiography of Malcolm X* by Alex Haley.

When they told me that I immediately bought the book and read it that night. I told them I had read it and they showed more trust in me. I was head of the Weed and Seed program at the White House at the time, and I wanted to get into some areas in the Washington D.C. area and see what was going on so I could do a more effective job.

So they took me around to where I wanted to go, including some of the bad areas of D.C. They knew what I was doing and wanted to help.

One day I said, "Lets go to Ana Costia Langston Terrace." They said, "We don't have any iron."

"What?" I said.

"We don't have any guns, if you don't have guns there you won't get any respect."

I learned a lot with Orlando and J.J., but most importantly they got me to read more about the life of Malcolm X and that led to the stamp.

The last two years of his life, Malcolm X was like Martin Luther King. He was non-violent, and preached to African Americans that they needed to go the way the Irish, Italians and Polish did when they came into this country. He said they needed to build their own networks, own communities, own corporations, work hard and invest in their companies.

So, when I proposed a Malcolm X stamp to the Citizens Stamp Advisory Committee there was a big discussion, and we got it approved.

The launch of the stamp was in Harlem where Malcolm X was killed. His daughters were there, but I couldn't attend because I was working at ESPN and it was in the middle of the NCAA Tournament. But they made sure to tell the Postal Service people to thank Digger for this day.

I look at that as one of the most significant stamps approved during my 22 years on the committee.

Father Ted and the Civil Rights Commission

Father Hesburgh was one of the original six on the Civil Rights Commission when he was appointed by President Dwight D. Eisenhower, the second of Father Ted's 16 presidential appointments. He was later made chairman of the Civil Rights Commission from 1969-72.

The commission was created on September 9, 1957 when Eisenhower signed the first Civil Rights Act passed by Congress in over 80 years. It was a tough battle in Congress to get it passed. There were many long filibusters on the subject, the most famous of which was led by South Carolina Senator Strom Thurmond who spoke for 24 hours and 18 minutes non-stop, still the longest filibuster by one person in history.

Finally the commission was approved and the six-person team was appointed by President Eisenhower. They were sworn in at the White House on January 2, 1958.

The committee included Hesburgh, John Battle, the former governor of Virginia, Doyle Carlton, the former governor of Florida, Robert Storey the dean of the SMU Law School, John Hannah, the president of Michigan State and former assistant secretary of defense, and Ernest Wilkins, the undersecretary of Labor and the only African American on the committee.

The Commission traveled all over the country, but mostly in the South, for two years and had hearings on basic civil rights issues ranging from voting rights to employment to education. The majority of the hearings in the south centered around voting rights.

There were counties in the South that didn't have a single African American registered to vote. That included Montgomery, Ala. where a county judge said he would burn the voting records before he turned them over to the commission. That local judge was George Wallace, who would go on to become Governor of the state of Alabama. The commission sent him a subpoena, and he eventually released the records.

The pure logistics of the travel became difficult because Wilkins, who had worked on the Manhattan Project and at 13 years old had been the youngest student in the history of the University of Chicago, was an African American.

For their first committee meeting in Montgomery in 1957 they could not find a hotel that would take them so they decided to go to the Maxwell Federal Air Base and stay at the bachelor officers' quarters.

"They first told us at Maxwell they could take the five white guys, but not the black, " said Father Ted. "John Hannah blew a fuse and called President Eisenhower. He told the President, 'You gave us a tough federal job and now we're at a federal air base and they won't even accept one of the members you appointed.'"

So President Eisenhower spoke to a general in an angry voice. "It may not have occurred to you, but 10 years ago, we desegregated the Armed Forces of the United States and we've desegregated everything else and I had to appoint a commission to pull it off."

He later said to the general, "Let me tell you something General, if they don't have a room and board in the next five minutes, you're going to be in Afghanistan tomorrow morning." He then hung up and that was the end of that.

Going to Land O' Lakes, Wisconsin

The commission was supposed to have its final hearing in 1959 in Shreveport, Louisiana. It was to be a three-day hearing and then the commission was going to stay three more days and write its final report. This was the final report that would go to Eisenhower with what would be the 12 major recommendations; recommendations that formed the foundation of the Civil Rights Act of 1964.

The members of the commission were all given a summons, which meant they were not going to be allowed to have a hearing in that city.

Father Ted sat in an uncomfortable room at

the Air Force Base wondering what they were going to do next. He knew one thing, this was not going to be an atmosphere that would lend itself to writing their final report for Eisenhower, never mind agreeing as a commission on any of the doctrines.

The next part of the story is another great example of the Power of Hesburgh, and why I consider him the Godfather of Civil Rights.

Father Ted called one of the Notre Dame longtime benefactors, A. O'Shaughnessy, and asked him if he could borrow his plane. He had a DC-3 that he used as a private plane.

"I've got the Civil Rights Commission here in Shreveport and they're ready to hang us or lynch us, and I've got to get them out of here," said Father Hesburgh.

He asked if O'Shaughnessy's plane could take the group to Land O'Lakes, Wisconsin to Notre Dame's retreat house.

Father Ted made special arrangements to get clearance for O'Shaughnessy's DC 3 to land at Maxwell in Shreveport. Civilian planes were not normally allowed there.

The plane arrived and the six members of the commission, plus their staff assistants, got on that plane for the five-and-a-half hour ride from Shreveport to Land O'Lakes.

Hesburgh sat on the floor in the back of the plane with the other members of the commission's assistants and began to summarize all the points that the group needed to make.

Now it was time for Hesburgh to be the diplomat and somehow get this commission of three Yankees and three Southerners, three democrats, two republicans and an independent (Hesburgh), to agree on the key points.

The first thing Hesburgh did before the plane even took off was to call ahead and arrange for a great dinner of steak, baked potatoes, apple pie a la mode and some dry martinis.

It was at the end of the dinner, that Hesburgh asked the group, "Do any of you like to fish?" All five hands went up in the air. So all six members got into three boats and went fishing. Hesburgh arranged for guides to take the men to the most plentiful areas and the group had the time of their lives.

They got back to the Notre Dame retreat house and had a meeting that started at about 10 p.m. The six commissioners and their respective lawyers sat down at a table on a screened in porch and went over 12 resolutions.

Everyone was in such a good mood from the meal and the fishing, that the first 11 resolutions passed unanimously. Even all the southern members of the commission were all in.

On the 12th resolution, which dealt with the integration of education, Governor Battle of Virginia asked the group if they would hate him for voting against it. The group told him to just vote his conscience, which he did, making the vote on the 12th resolution 5-1.

Days later when the commission met at the Oval Office with President Eisenhower who had the 12 resolutions in hand, the President said he was surprised that the commission had agreed upon such tough resolutions by unanimous vote in all but one resolution.

He asked them how they had come to an agreement of any kind. Father Hesburgh replied, "You didn't put three Republicans and three Democrats on this commission, you put six fisherman on this commission and we wrote it in Land O'Lakes, Wisconsin after a terrific night of fishing."

Eisenhower said he needed to think about putting more fishermen on commissions. He then asked Father Ted if he could someday go to Notre Dame's retreat house to do some fishing himself. Hesburgh said, "of course."

By the end of his presidency he took advantage of the opportunity and they brought the Wisconsin fish back to the White House and presented them to the White House Chef for preparation.

That final meeting of the Commission at Land O'Lakes took place in 1959, but it was July 2, 1964 before the Civil Rights Act was adopted.

Eisenhower's second term ended in January

of 1961 and he gave the documents to his successor President John F. Kennedy. It was Kennedy's plan to have it adopted as a second term proposal. It was believed at the time that pushing such a proposal would be political suicide in the South and Kennedy would not get re-elected in 1964.

The vote between Kennedy and Nixon in 1960 was close as it was and with Democrats holding a majority in the South at the time, Kennedy and his advisors thought it was best to make it a second term project.

But, Kennedy was assassinated on November 22, 1963 and Lyndon Johnson became president.

Johnson thought he might be president for just a year and a month, but he felt he could establish a lasting legacy in his short time by passing the Civil Rights Bill. It was his goal to desegregate the country. So he went after it.

Johnson was the consummate politician in Father Hesburgh's eyes and that was certainly the case in regards to this bill. Father Ted held Johnson in high regard for his work in Civil Rights, especially considering he was from the state of Texas.

When President Johnson had his first meeting with Congress, he walked in with one document in his hand and it was the proposed Civil Rights Bill. It was the top item on his agenda. According to Father Hesburgh he told them they were going to vote for his law, and he slapped the bill on the table with authority.

At the beginning, published reports felt that Johnson didn't have a third of the votes needed to pass the bill. But he knew each of them in the room personally (Senate and House). He challenged them publically, then called them privately.

According to Father Hesburgh, "He started calling them at 3 a.m. and woke them out of a sound sleep. One of the Senators answered the phone and said, 'Mr. President are we at war?'

"Johnson said, 'Yes, you could say we are at war—a war about human rights and what kind of country America is going to be.'"

In those late phone calls Johnson actually threatened to ruin them politically. "If you don't vote for it, I'll make sure you won't get re-elected because you won't get funding for your causes."

While he got a lot of help from Presidents Eisenhower and Johnson, Father Hesburgh was the Godfather of Civil Rights in this country. Some would say that his work and the results of that work years later was miraculous.

The Civil Rights Bill was formally approved on July 2, 1964. There is some magnitude in that Father Ted died just seven months after the 50-year anniversary of the establishment of that bill.

Father Ted stayed on the commission until 1972. He made a point of expanding their causes and made the point that these rules were not just for the cause of African Americans, but for all people regardless of race and nationality.

As chairman of the commission he authorized a review of the Civil Rights practices of the federal government. The results, which were based on hiring statistics, were not favorable. Of the 40 different departments that were investigated, the commission gave a "poor" grade to 39 of them.

This did not sit well with President Richard Nixon, who had once offered Father Hesburgh the opportunity to direct the country's war on poverty. As a result, while Father Ted was in Washington at a Civil Rights meeting, Nixon sent word through a messenger that he wanted all six members of the current commission to resign.

Father Hesburgh followed Nixon's request and cleaned out his Washington office.

In the years since those original resolutions were developed by Father Ted and the Civil Rights Commission, he took pride in seeing the progress minorities made in the country. He took pride in the success of Condoleezza Rice, a graduate from Notre Dame's MBA school, who became Secretary of State, and the election of our first African American President, Barack Obama.

But, he took more pride in seeing the success stories of African American students at Notre Dame. When Rice spoke at Father Ted's memorial service she mentioned the day that Father Ted called her to let her know that Notre Dame had its first African American valedictorian (Katie Washington, 2010).

Coaching the Streets

Working with Orlando and J.J., that was all a part of "Coaching the Streets." Father Hesburgh always told me, right until the final week of his life, "Don't stop coaching the streets."

Working on the Weed and Seed program with President George H.W. Bush in the White House after the end of my coaching career, was a perfect example. As I said before, Father Hesburgh motivated me to do more with our "What have you really been doing" talk we had in his office.

It was work I know Father Hesburgh was proud of and you could say it was a by-product of his work with Civil Rights. Weed meant going into a neighborhood with as many federal, state and local agents as possible and taking out the bad element.

The bridge from weed to seed was community policing, which meant establishing neighborhood watch groups. The neighborhoods started a team watching their area in a partnership with police, who we asked to get out of the squad cars and go on foot patrols and bicycle patrols and identify the bad element.

Seed meant economic empowerment. It was about getting businesses to come into these neighborhoods and stimulate economic growth.

Start a business in the neighborhood, give them some infrastructure, no taxes and give these people a way to succeed.

In New Orleans for example, we went to public housing and found the three best women who could make gumbo. We got a person who could run a restaurant to coach them on how to run a catering business where they could cater lunches for conventions in New Orleans.

We got them working and running their own business. And with that type of lunch business they still had time to get home by 4 p.m. and be with their kids.

There was another example in Trenton, N.J. where we kept schools open until 9 p.m. We fed them lunch and dinner. We had strong after school programs for them where we reinforced what they had learned during the day and had them look at career options. We took field trips to get them interested in different professions that give them goals to work towards.

A few years ago I got involved with the community and started a basketball program at the Kroc Center to get kids off the streets.

I would go to them one-on-one and say, "Come here. You go to the Crossings and you are going to find hope. You are going to get faith and you are going to get your GED. Once you get that GED, you go next door to the Career Academy. You can become an electrician and make $60-70,000 a year."

This is what "Coaching the Streets" was all about. Save one person and that person can save 100.

One day I went to see Father Ted and he asked me, "So, how is it going, coaching the streets?" I looked at him and said, "Well, I'm not Duarte yet, but I'm getting close."

That's why Father Ted told me the last week I was with him, "Digger, keep coaching the streets."

Hesburgh and Hawkins

Father Ted had a special relationship with Tom Hawkins. A native of Chicago, Hawkins was a scholarship basketball player who came to Notre Dame in the fall of 1955. He was not the first African American basketball player at Notre Dame. Joe Bertrand and Entee Shine were the first when they enrolled as freshmen in 1951.

Hawkins became a star of the basketball

Father Ted and Tom Hawkins had a close relationship from the time he moved into campus in 1955.

team and helped the Irish to the NCAA Tournament his junior and senior years when he was named an All-American. The 1958 team finished with a 24-5 record and reached the Elite Eight of the NCAA Tournament.

He finished his career averaging 23 points and 17 rebounds a game over three years and he still holds the Notre Dame career rebounding record nearly 60 years after he played his last game. When he was named an All-American in 1958, he became the first Notre Dame African American athlete to be honored as a first-team All-American in any sport.

In an interview for this book, Hawkins recalled that Father Hesburgh made a special effort for him to feel welcome and even came to Cavanaugh Hall with some other administrators and coaches when he first arrived to meet him and his family. At the time there were only 10 African Americans on campus and Hawkins was the only African American in any of his classes for four years.

"Segregation was the name of the game across the country when I first came to Notre Dame, but inside the cocoon of the Notre Dame campus I didn't feel that at all," said Hawkins.

"There was a feeling of freedom and dignity compared to other schools and that was because of Father Hesburgh.

"Father Ted had told the world that if a minority was not welcomed at your establishment, then Notre Dame was not welcomed."

During his sophomore year, Hawkins went to an Italian restaurant in South Bend and was turned away.

"When I walked in they asked me if I had a reservation," recalled Hawkins. "A reservation? No one had a reservation at this restaurant, you just walked in.

"When the other Notre Dame students in the restaurant saw I had been refused a seat, they all got up and left."

Hesburgh learned of the incident and made it known that no Notre Dame student was to go to that restaurant until Hawkins was given an apology and allowed to eat there.

About two weeks later, Hawkins had a visitor in his dorm room.

"There was a knock on my door late one afternoon and it was Paul Hornung.

'Damn you Hawk,' he said with a smile. 'Because of you I can't get my favorite pizza. Come on, we are going downtown to straighten this out.'"

So the two of them went to the pizza restaurant. Hornung had talked to the owner and convinced him that he needed to make an apology to Hawkins and let the African Americans eat there. Having won the Heisman and been the face of Notre Dame sports for the last three years, Horning had some power and could be very persuasive.

"We walked in and the owner made the apology right away and seated us. Then Paul and I had a large pizza."

Hawkins and Hornung remained friends and when Hornung was inducted into the Pro Football Hall of Fame, Hawkins had him as a guest on his radio program in Los Angeles.

"We talked about that story and I told him, 'Paul, you didn't have to do that.'"

"Hornung responded, 'Oh yes I did.'

"And, he meant it. "

He did it for more than just wanting to eat their pizza.

"It was the right thing to do," said Hornung.

Hawkins and Hesburgh remained close over the years. Every time Hawkins returned to campus he went by to see him for a visit at his office in the Golden Dome or the 13th floor of the library.

When Hawkins went back to campus for his 50-year reunion in 2009, he had a meeting with Father Ted. Both had surprise gifts for the other. Hesburgh had arranged to get an 8X10 print of Hawkins playing in a game for Notre Dame. It was a picture of Hawkins dunking in a game against Bradley in the Chicago Stadium that had been in the 1958 Dome. Hesburgh told him it was his favorite picture of Hawkins.

Hawkins then surprised Father Hesburgh with a picture of Hesburgh inside a frame that also had a poem Hawkins had written. It was entitled, "The House of Hesburgh."

"Welcome to the House of Hesburgh. It has no walls and yet is a fortress of humanity, intelligence and dignity. It is a bastion of religiosity with windows open to the world. It is a place that you can go to restore your faith, talk and listen to your soul, chart your life's course and fortify yourself for the road ahead.

"This home is filled with the love of God and our sacred Mother. It is a storehouse of forthright conviction, understanding and safe advice honed by years of education, fervent prayer and effective living.

"It is well decorated with mementos of an eclectic

past. It features an endless array of both national and international awards and photographs documenting a life of historic accomplishments. It is a place where the echoes of the past miraculously blend with the hope of the future.

"This wonderful homestead is landscaped with the beautiful flowers of spring, the green leaves of summer, the radiant change of colors of the fall and tinged with the blustery winds and swirling snows of winter. It is in every respect a place that stirs your being and inspires the spirit within you.

"As you leave please go in peace, and upon departing, know that you have experienced the wonders of God through one of the most powerful and enlightened vicars of our time. Rest assured you will never forget that you have visited the House of Hesburgh.

"By the time I finished reading the poem, tears were coming down Father's cheek and when I saw those tears I started to cry. It was just the two of us in his Library office.

'Darn you Tom Hawkins, I don't cry.'

"That was a magic moment for me and I know it meant a lot to Father Ted. With all the great awards he received and special people he met, he put that framed poem on display in his office."

Hawkins was inducted into the Notre Dame basketball Ring of Honor in January of 2015, just six weeks before Father Ted died. They met for the last time on that visit. Notre Dame's athletic video department followed Hawkins to that meeting and in the video you can hear Father Ted say, "This is one of our greatest graduates."

Andrew Young on Hesburgh's Impact on Civil Rights Commission

Andrew Young was a young civil rights leader of the time and worked with Martin Luther King in that cause in the 1960s. During a video Notre Dame produced on Father Ted's life in 2007, he talked about the credibility Father Hesburgh gave to the commission and the cause.

"The key to the success of the Civil Rights Movement was to keep it from being a radical leftist movement and recognize that it was truly a movement coming out of the Judeo-Christian U.S. Constitutional tradition of justice.

"Well, nobody could represent all of those forces like Father Ted could. And, he did it in such a quiet unassuming, non-judgmental way that when he was with you, you didn't have to worry about who was against you."

Below is a summary of the 11 resolutions that were adopted in the Civil Rights Act of 1964. Most of these resolutions were from the original report (original report had 12) Hesburgh and the Civil Rights Commission wrote at Notre Dame's Retreat facility in Land O'Lakes, Wisconsin in 1959.

Title I
Barred unequal application of voter registration requirements.

Title II
Outlawed discrimination based on race, color, religion or national origin in hotels, motels, restaurants, theaters, and all other public accommodations engaged in interstate commerce; exempted private clubs without defining the term "private"

Title III
Prohibited state and municipal governments from denying access to public facilities on grounds of race, color, religion or national origin.

Title IV
Encouraged the desegregation of public schools and authorized the U.S. Attorney General to file suits to enforce said act.

Title V

Expanded the Civil Rights Commission established by the earlier Civil Rights Act of 1957 with additional powers, rules and procedures.

Title VI

Prevented discrimination by government agencies that receive federal funds. If an agency is found in violation of Title VI, that agency may lose its federal funding.

Title VII

Prohibits discrimination against an individual because of his or her association with another individual of a particular race, color, religion, sex, or national origin, such as by an interracial marriage.

Title VIII

Required compilation of voter-registration and voting data in geographic areas specified by the Commission on Civil Rights.

Title IX

Made it easier to move civil rights cases from state courts with segregationist judges and all white juries to federal court. This was of crucial importance to civil rights activists who contended that they could not get fair trials in state courts

Title X

Established the Community Relations Service, tasked with assisting in community disputes involving claims of discrimination.

Title XI

Gave a defendant accused of certain categories of criminal contempt in a matter arising under title II, III, IV, V, VI, or VII of the Act the right to a jury trial. If convicted, the defendant can be fined an amount not to exceed $1,000 or imprisoned for not more than six months.

CHAPTER 6
RUNNING NOTRE DAME

His Greatest Accomplishment

One day I was in Father Ted's office on the 13th floor of the Hesburgh Library and I asked him, "What is your greatest accomplishment in your time at Notre Dame."

Father Ted was standing at his window looking at Our Lady on the Dome and said, "We are now 50 percent coed."

That was one of his major goals in the middle of his presidency and I was fascinated to hear him say that. When you look at all he has accomplished, that was the first thing he said and there was no hesitation.

Coeducation finally happened at Notre Dame in the fall of 1972 when 125 freshman and 275 upperclassmen women were admitted. Today Notre Dame receives nearly 20,000 applicants and accepts 2,000 in a typical freshman class. Approximately, a thousand are men and a thousand are women.

It took a while to get there. For the first 20 years of Father Ted's presidency it was an all male school. That bothered him. He felt Notre Dame was a world class experience, but only half of the world was allowed to benefit from that experience.

The process started in the late 1960s. Father Ted and the Board of Trustees thought the easiest way to accomplish coeducation was to merge with St. Mary's College, the all women

Catholic school across highway 31 from Notre Dame.

That process proved to be difficult as St. Mary's College administrators came to the conclusion that they would lose their identity. Just like Notre Dame, it was a school that was proud of its traditions and heritage.

When Father Ted realized this was the case, he told many that he understood their feelings. "They wanted to date us, but didn't want to marry us."

So in 1970 it was announced that Notre Dame would add the proper number of dormitories and other infrastructure to admit women for the fall of 1972. (Everything but the laundry that is…Notre Dame men were still able to send their clothes each week to the laundry, but the women did it themselves.)

I remember talking to Father Ted about bringing Condoleezza Rice back to Notre Dame to run the Hesburgh International Peace Studies Program. "Can you imagine if we got her back here to run that program?" I told him. "All of a sudden, we've got Israel and Palestine sitting down at a table at Notre Dame."

I know he doubted she would leave Stanford at this point in her career, but the mere thought of the possibilities brought a smile to Father Ted's face as he considered how far we had come since he became president in 1952.

Hesburgh the Marketer

Father Ted knew how to market, and he did it in a very similar manner to the way Knute Rockne marketed Notre Dame football in the 1920s.

Rockne was a genius. He put together the series with Southern California starting in 1927 that brought attention to his program on the west coast. And he had games in Chicago at Soldier's field, where 127,000 fans once saw a Notre Dame vs. Southern Cal game, the most ever to see a college game until 2016. And, he brought the team to Yankee Stadium to play Army.

In 1929, Notre Dame played all their home games in Chicago while Notre Dame Stadium was being built. Rockne was a risk taker and building a 59,000-seat stadium in little South Bend, Ind. during the depression took a lot of guts. Of course, playing the 1929 season in Chicago helped create the strong alumni and subway alumni base we see today.

It was Rockne's idea to market Notre Dame on a national basis through radio. In the late 1920s radio stations from New York broadcast Notre Dame football games and Rockne didn't charge them to do it. He realized the benefits that were going to come from being the only college football team on the air waves in New York. That soon led to a national network.

Rockne had a national view of Notre Dame, which is amazing when you look at the fact that where the school is geographically and for much of his career the country was in difficult economic times.

Similarly, Father Hesburgh marketed Notre Dame nationally, and then on a worldwide basis, and from that concept is what we see today.

Notre Dame is the ultimate national school. Rockne started with national radio and we started the national replay network with Lindsey Nelson and Paul Hornung when Father Ted was president.

And, of course, Father Hesburgh took that national scope when it came to the university, whether it was the recruitment of professors, or in fundraising.

All of his outside work, whether it was as a member of 16 presidential commissions, or being on the board of major corporations, or traveling the world to seek a solution to world hunger, brought a global scope to Notre Dame that no other school had.

Hesburgh never stopped raising money for Notre Dame and continued that national marketing approach. I remember coming to see him at his office in the Hesburgh Library when Father Ted was in his 90s. Coming out of his office were a couple of development people and a woman who looked like a fundraising prospect.

She knew me—I didn't know her—but I knew of her. She came here for one reason, to meet Father Hesburgh. She left and a $10 million dollar check was going to Notre Dame development the next week. But that was the power of Hesburgh until the day he died. And quite frankly that power still exists today.

Father Hesburgh and Father Joyce took the concepts of Rockne in the 1920s and molded all the aspects of Notre Dame into what it is today. They marketed Notre Dame nationally, and they found a way to raise funds by creating relationships with people that were of great resource to Notre Dame. They had a dream to make it the best Catholic university in the world and one of the best universities in the country.

As a result, today we see Notre Dame as a top 20 institution nationally among public or private schools. The Mendoza Business School has been ranked number one or two by Bloomberg Business the last five years.

Joan Kroc

Father Ted and Father Joyce had a vision as to how to raise money and get people involved with the school. They successfully convinced people to become involved in the mission of Notre Dame.

But sometimes the relationships weren't recruited, they just happened naturally from Hesburgh being Hesburgh.

In 1987, Father Ted was invited to speak at a luncheon on issues facing the country including poverty, jobs, and help in some other lower income areas. After the speech, a women came to Father Ted and said, "How can I get involved Father?"

Father Ted spoke with her, and after she left, he asked the priest who had asked him to speak, "Who was that lady?"

The priest replied, "That was Joan Kroc."

Father Ted said to the priest, "Who is Joan Kroc?"

The priest replied, "McDonalds, you know, hamburgers."

Father Ted didn't know that the Kroc family owned McDonalds. So, he followed up with some correspondence and phone calls and invited her to the Southern California football game in South Bend that October.

He gave her a personal tour around campus in a golf cart that weekend. "This is O'Shaughnessy Hall, the current building for The College of Arts and Letters," he said as they toured campus. He showed her Haggar Hall, the business administration building at the time.

Father Ted also told her of his vision for an International Peace Institute on campus and his plan to use O'Shaughnessy, Haggar and other buildings for various aspects of the project.

Kroc said to Hesburgh, "You don't have one building for all of this together?" Father Ted replied that we did not.

Kroc then returned home and promptly sent Father Ted a check for $10 million so he could have that Peace Institute in one building.

That next spring (1988) they had a ground breaking ceremony for the facility with shovels and pictures of Mrs. Kroc and Father Ted.

After a year, no bricks had been laid in the ground and Father Hesburgh was a bit upset. So he went over to the development office, and asked, "What is one year's interest on $10 million."

Back then it was 10 percent. "Send a check for $1 million to Joan Kroc because we haven't put a brick in the ground yet."

That got things going.

For one of his later birthdays, Father Ted went to the Land O' Lakes facility in Wisconsin in May. He liked to go there that time of the year, to unwind after graduation, and fish. She called him and said, "Father, did you get my birthday card?"

He had not, but said he would get it when he went back to campus. When he went through his mail he opened the card and in it was a check for $25 million.

The building was built fairly quickly after that.

Today, The Hesburgh Center for International Studies houses the Kroc Institute for International Peace Studies and the Kellogg Institute for International Studies.

The facility is right on Notre Dame Avenue as you make the drive towards the Golden Dome. After her death in 2003 the Kroc Foundation gave Notre Dame another $50 million.

Father Ted Keeps His Cool

In the early 1970s I got a call from a guy named Don Kelly, a businessman in Chicago who did not go to Notre Dame, but was a big Notre Dame fan. He grew up in Chicago. He wanted to play golf with me at Butler National in Chicago, at the time one of the best golf courses in the Midwest. It was the home of the PGA Tour's Western Open at the time. I could play pretty well at that time.

So we became good friends. In 1975 we opened the football season at Boston College on a Monday night and I wanted to go. I told Don I would get the four tickets if he got the plane. It was Dan Devine's first game as head coach. Kelly loved Notre Dame football, but he was not a big fan of Dan Devine.

A year or so later, I thought Don would

be a good person to have on the Notre Dame Business Council. So, I got Jim Gibbons to set a up meeting with Father Hesburgh at the Morris Inn.

At the time, things were getting a little hot for Coach Devine, so I told Don not to bring him up at our conversation. Father Hesburgh always gave his coaches five years and he wanted to support his coach.

I was afraid that if Don was real negative about Devine it might hurt his chances of getting on the Business Council.

I told him before the meeting, "Don't bring up Dan Devine."

Sure enough, five minutes into the dinner, he brought up Devine. Jim Gibbons and I looked at each other and had an "Oh my God," moment.

But Father Ted kept his cool and we got through the dinner.

A few years later, Don became the President of Esmart Corporation and was on the Notre Dame Board of Trustees and eventually gave $6 million to the Business School. He paid for a new wing.

Hesburgh's Open Window Policy

Father Hesburgh was on the road a lot, but when he was in town, he was there for the students. He believed in working on these world projects and presidential commissions, "whenever I could bring fruit back to campus."

All a student had to do was knock on his door and ask to see him. Helen would check his schedule. "Father, a student is here from New Mexico, and would like to see you for a couple of minutes."

She would usually tell the student to wait a few minutes and then Father Ted would speak with the student.

It was well known around campus that if Father Hesburgh's light was on in his office in the Dome you could approach him with a problem. Sometimes students would climb the fire escape outside his office after midnight and knock on the window in hopes of some late night consultation.

I always told students when I met them, even after he retired, "You need to go by and see Father Ted. It is a part of the Notre Dame experience. Don't leave this place without getting a blessing from him as you get ready for the game of life after Notre Dame."

Everyone Together in the ACC

Father Ted understood progress, but he also understood the importance of relationships and working together through personal interaction.

One of the things he liked about the Athletic and Convocation Center he designed with Father Joyce in 1968, was that all the coaches, all the administrators and most of the locker rooms were in one building.

There was interaction between the head coaches and that was good for the camaraderie, the spirit of the department. On the first floor of the Convocation Center my office was in one corner and Ara Parseghian's office was in the other. When I was a young coach in 1971, and needed some advice, I just had to walk 60 feet down the hall to walk into Ara's office.

As the department has grown, it has been more and more difficult to continue this approach. In his retirement, when we drove by the athletic facilities, Father Ted worried when he saw new buildings going up that they were going to separate the sports. I know he felt that way when the new football facility, the Guglielmino Complex, was being built because it separated the football coaches, players and administration from the rest of the department.

I know he felt that way about his administration and wanted to keep as many people in the Dome as possible.

When you look at who he was, he could walk into a room and people would just know he was there. You would brace up your level of respect. He had an aura about him. He was a person who people held in the highest respect whether it was with the faculty, the students, administration or the landscapers on campus.

That was a result of his personal contact.

He believed in the family, and he sold the Notre Dame family. As a Notre Dame coach or employee in any department, you developed those relationships through interaction in your job each day. And it helped that he had the wardrobe of a priest.

When he knew there were things to be done, he would listen to faculty, deans, staff and students. What's it going to take to make it better for you at Notre Dame? Then he would go out and get it done.

He made this place better for today because of his personal communication with those around him. Where do we go next and how do we get it done? That was a major part of his leadership style.

Hesburgh the Risk Taker

What was Hesburgh's leadership style? Well, what is leadership?

Leadership is creativity.

When you look at Father Ted's career, he was a big-time risk taker. Even though he was a priest and always was a priest, he was street smart, he was a survivor and he had no ego. He had many situations where he was challenged, but he knew how to survive. In the 1960s there was much unrest on campuses around the country. He faced the problem at

Notre Dame head on, and gave protesters that prevented the University and students from doing their normal activities, 15 minutes of reflection before ending their protest.

Otherwise, they were gone. It worked. There were many times he was challenged or given strong recommendations by the Board of Trustees. Ed Stephen was the first Chairman of the Board of Trustees who was a lay person. There were only about 12 on the board then. Ed would make a suggestion and sometimes Father Ted would say, "Ed, I know what you are saying and where you are coming from, but we are going to do it this way." He had great respect for the Board of Trustees, after all, he was the reason the board moved away from being all clergy in 1967.

That was Father Ted being a risk taker, but he was also a survivor, because he knew what he wanted and went after it. And that's leadership.

Creativity, risk taker, street smarts, and survivor were his most important characteristics in being a leader of this campus.

And, as a disciple of Hesburgh, I would teach my players those characteristics and they used that in their life after basketball.

You can look at John Paxson, and his years in management with the Chicago Bulls, you look at Stan Wilcox as the athletic director at Florida

State, you look at Scott Paddock as the President of Chicago Speedway and Jamere Jackson, who has been the Chief Financial Officer for Nielsen Corporation since 2014.

All of those players benefitted from leadership qualities that Father Hesburgh taught all of us during his time as president.

The Importance of the Undergraduate Education

Father Ted always had a sense for the long term importance of the undergraduate education. I can think of many examples where my former players benefitted from it.

Take a kid like Mike Mitchell, who back in 1979 was a freshman for our team. He tore the same knee as a sophomore and junior. He came back for his senior year and I made him a captain. He played with John Paxson.

San Francisco came here as a top 10 team in 1982 and we beat them thanks to Mike's best game. He had overcome so much, but stuck with it, showed leadership, creativity and was a survivor. So I gave him the game ball, the only time I gave a game ball to a player in 20 years.

After Notre Dame he became the president of Nestles USA Beverage Company and is one of my most successful former players. He graduated with a C+ average GPA in business, but he made the most of his undergraduate experience here and is a great representative of this school.

I also look at Jay Jordan, who was a football player. He didn't play much football, but was on the team. He graduated and started his life in the business world with his own company, Jordan Industries. A couple of years ago he gave $30 million to the Notre Dame School of Science and it is now named after him.

Jay and I are great friends. I saw him one day after the Jordan School of Science was finished. "Why would you give $30 million for a science building? You don't even know what H_2O means!"

And we would laugh…But that's what Notre Dame was. And those are the type of people that came here, lived the Notre Dame experience and became ultra successful.

We all know somebody who has always been an A+ student. But you become a winner after you have had an F and you deal with it. That's when you're a winner in the game of life.

So to be a successful leader, give me someone who has creativity, someone who is a risk taker, someone who is street smart and someone who is a survivor. Notre Dame, under Hesburgh, cultivated those qualities in their undergraduates. That was an important mission for Hesburgh, to make his students prepared for the real world and to be contributors to that world.

You've got to do a little more work in the application process to find these people. I don't care if they've got the highest test scores. The game of life is not about test scores. Father Hesburgh believed that too.

The Importance of Community Service

Community Service was always at the forefront of the Notre Dame experience under Father Hesburgh. You didn't just come here and go to the library every night for five hours. We have shown throughout this book that Father Ted was a leader in Civil Rights and serving others, fighting world hunger and many other human rights issues.

He wanted Notre Dame students to become involved. It is really a Notre Dame tradition that dates to the founding of the school and Father Sorin's desire to form Catholic parishes in this area.

When I arrived at Notre Dame in 1971, Father Ted was in his 19th year as president. It was already a center for social concerns. There was a neighborhood help study program which meant Notre Dame students were going out in the community and helping students in grammar school, middle school and high school with their courses, especially core courses: English, math, science, history, even reading and writing skills.

Today, there is the Robinson Community Learning Center on Eddy Street. It used to be an A&P grocery store. One of the many programs is Shakespeare, which is taught by Notre Dame students. They do a play at the end of the year, just to show kids other options in the game of life, as actors.

There is also the Alliance for Catholic Education program, run by Father Tim Scully. That is a terrific program where graduates work for two years at an inner city Catholic school and make a difference in kids' lives. They tell kids about biology, engineering and many other subjects so these kids have a goal. Most of them don't know what is out there.

Today, they have over 80 percent of the Notre Dame student body doing some type of community service, whether it's here in South Bend, or elsewhere in the United States or across the world.

To give you an example, the men's soccer team a few of years ago was mentoring at the Pearly School, a grammar school right down the street from Notre Dame's campus. Two years ago that same team went to Africa for three weeks to an area where AIDS is still prevalent, to teach kids how to play soccer and do other educational projects with them. They made a difference in their lives and used soccer as a connection.

Those were all projects that Father Hesburgh took pride in when he learned of the community service work Notre Dame students were doing. It is all about providing hope for a community.

Father Ted believed that was part of the mission at Notre Dame. Once you leave here, wherever you end up, you have to become a community leader through action, not just words.

Surround yourself by putting together a team of assets that can take one of the issues in that community and make it change from a negative to a positive. That's always been a part of what Notre Dame has been from Day 1 and it is a tradition that Hesburgh continued for his 35 years as president, and in his 28 years of retirement.

CHAPTER 7
THE SPIRITUALITY OF THE HIDDEN CRUCIFIX

The Spirit of Hesburgh at Notre Dame

Father Hesburgh had a way of making you believe in yourself, making you believe that you have the physical, mental and spiritual direction to make a change for the better in the world.

He had a belief in himself, and that was the reason he was able to convey that to others. He said to me and to many others, that he knew when he was six years old he wanted to become a priest.

He was never distracted from that to the point where he said Mass every day of his life as a priest, including his final day. And he went to extremes at times to do it. In some foreign countries he actually snuck wine into some countries in his mouth wash bottle in his travel bag to use at Mass.

There is a spirituality at Notre Dame that goes back to the beginning.

The French priests, the Congregation of the Sacred Cross (C.S.C.) had this vision to come to the United States and start a school. When Father Edward Sorin went to Vincennes to see the Bishop, he said there was land in South Bend, Indiana with a big lake with a marsh and a log cabin next to it.

The Bishop told Father Sorin that is where he should go because there is already a missionary there.

So the C.S.C. brothers and nuns made

the journey to South Bend in 1842 and they lived in that log cabin. In 1842, they took clay from the lake, made bricks and constructed the building next to the log cabin and called it "Old College". That was Notre Dame in its beginning.

People can't believe it when I give a campus tour and tell them that story. "And, there it is, the log cabin. There is Old College. That was the beginning of Notre Dame and basically 'The Spirit of Notre Dame'."

From that moment in 1842 and 1843 until what we saw with Father Hesburgh for 35 years, that was the spirituality that still drives me, drives Notre Dame students, drives Notre Dame administrators and professors today. It has been a carry over from the Blessed Mother, Jesus, and Mary Magdalene to this place.

The university is officially called Notre Dame du lac, or Our Lady by the Lake. To me it is no different than the Grotto of Lourdes in Lourdes, France or Fatima or Medjugorje, where the Blessed Mother appeared.

The Hidden Crucifix

I am a great believer in the Hidden Crucifix at Notre Dame and to me it is the greatest example of spirituality on the campus.

It is a major part of the sacred turf on this campus. I am not sure how long it has been here (see sidebar at end of this chapter), but it is the end of a walking trail for the Stations of the Cross.

To get there you go past Columba Hall on the way to St. Mary's College and bear right by the cemetery. Follow the road down Seminary Drive and it is off to the right. You will see the Stations of the Cross, and the Hidden Crucifix is at the end of the path up a short hill protected by woods. You can see it more clearly in the winter time, even with the snow.

At the top of the area is the life-sized bronze statue of Jesus hanging from the cross, flanked by the statue of Mary on the right and a statue of Mary Magdalene on the left.

I first discovered it during my first season as head coach (1971) and used to walk my dogs on campus, but I didn't think that much about it until I read *The Da Vinci Code* and talked to Father Hesburgh about it.

Father Ted told me about the importance the Hidden Crucifix had in his major decisions on this campus. He took many walks there from his office in the Golden Dome (administration building) when he had an important decision to make.

You would be surprised at the number of students who spend four years here and don't know where it is. True, it doesn't jump out at you, but if you come to Notre Dame, you have

Picture 1: 6:30 p.m., June 17, 2008

Picture 2: 6:40 p.m., June 17, 2008

Picture 3: 6:50 p.m., June 17, 2008

to include it on the campus tour. I always do when I give my tour.

The Crown of Thorns

On June 17, 2008 while standing in front of the Hidden Crucifix I took pictures of the sunset at 6:30 p.m., 6:40 p.m. and 6:50 p.m. It was a breathtaking image.

In the 6:50 p.m. photo there was a glow around the Hidden Crucifix. I got the pictures developed at a CVS store in South Bend, and when I came in to pick them up the lady behind the counter was very excited. "You've got to see this," she said when I walked in the door.

For Linda's birthday (August 1, 2008), we went to New York and stopped by to see Leroy Neiman, the famous artist, who encouraged me to become an artist in 1990. I am a Vincent Van Gogh-Matisse freak.

I met him at a function at the White House for the National Physical Fitness Day under George H.W. Bush.

During the meeting at his apartment, I showed Leroy and his wife Janet the pictures I had taken at the Hidden Crucifix back in June. His wife Janet looked at the pictures and said, " It's the Crown of Thorns."

When I returned, I blew the pictures up and took them to Father Ted. He said almost immediately, "The Crown of Thorns."

They Knew

I was at the Hidden Crucifix on April 28, 2010 and at 11 a.m., I received a call on my cell. It was from Doctor Mark Toth, who had the results of a biopsy I had taken because I had been suffering from symptoms that could indicate I had prostate cancer.

Sure enough, Dr. Toth said the biopsy confirmed that I had prostate cancer. I looked at the Blessed Mother, Mary Magdalene and Jesus on the Cross and said, "The three of you knew, huh. That's why you got me here today."

Finding out at the Hidden Crucifix was a wake up call. It was as if the three of them were telling me to get going and get this taken care of.

So, immediately, I called my daughter Karen Moyer, who was out in Seattle because her husband, Jamie Moyer, was pitching for the Seattle Mariners. Karen and Jamie were both on the board at the Fred Hutchinson Cancer Research Center in Seattle, Washington. The Hutchinson Cancer Research Center was a leader when it came to the Da Vinci Robotic Surgery.

My surgeons were Dr. Bill Ellis, a Stanford graduate, and Dr. Jonathan Wright, a Boston College graduate. I busted them about their football programs at the time. Notre Dame was playing both schools that next fall. In fact, Dr.

Ellis came to the Stanford game that October. They did the robotic surgery. It was supposed to take a couple of weeks to get the results back. It was June 11 and Linda and I were at Karen's house in Seattle recovering and we were watching Jamie pitch in Boston for the Mariners.

My cell phone rang as we were watching the game, and it was Dr. Ellis. Jamie was not doing well at Fenway. The Green Monster was going to need a paint job after this game.

The first thing Dr. Ellis said was, "You can have two beers tonight."

I said, "Yeah, you watching Moyer too? "

He said, "No, your biopsy from Tuesday, June 8 came back. The lymph nodes outside are clean. There's no more cancer! "

Every organ in our bodies has four layers of protection, except our pancreas. My cancer got in the third layer, but never broke through the fourth. So it had not spread to other organs.

I called Karen and left her a message. Friday, June 11th, at 8:26 p.m. - "Heard the great news!!! Will take that for eight runs any day."

We had to stay in Seattle a few more days as I recovered from the surgery, but we got on a plane on June 17 and flew back to South Bend.

We wanted to get back on that exact date because that was the two-year anniversary to the day I had taken the Crown of Thorns picture at the Hidden Crucifix (June 17, 2008).

6:50 p.m., June 17, 2010.
Two years later I returned to give thanks.

They cleared me to fly that June 17, and when we landed, Dr. Fred Ferlic (Notre Dame physician for many years) and his wife Mary Jane picked Linda and me up and we went straight to the Hidden Crucifix and gave our prayers of thanksgiving.

What else can I say, I was suppose to be there.

Digger, What took you so long

I did a painting of a crucifix in 2009 and I took it to show Father Hesburgh in his office. The painting had the three holy women around

The Five Wounds of Jesus, my painting. . . .The Five Wounds of Jesus crucifix from Jerusalem.

the crucifix like it was Good Friday. The three were Mary, the wife of Clopas, Mary, the mother of Jesus, and Mary Magdalene.

I called them the four holy women because I had a pregnant Mary Magdalene in the picture. She was pregnant with Sarah. Father Ted looked at the painting and said, "There was no hanky-panky back then. " I never laughed so hard. That was a side of him that few people saw. He had a great sense of humor.

He blessed the painting, signed it, and dated it (9-18-2009) on the back. I proudly said, "Father, I started painting back in 1990 and this is my first religious painting. He just looked at me and took the cigar out of his mouth and said,

"What took you so long?"

That was Father Ted at his best.

The painting I did of the three holy Women had a yellow circle around the crucifix. I didn't know why.

In July 2013, while coaching the Canadian Maccabiah Games team in Israel, I bought a crucifix in Jerusalem. It was called the "Five Wounds of Jesus." There were two for his hands, two for his feet and one for the side wound.

I couldn't believe it. You'll see it in the picture of my painting and the crucifix from Jerusalem. I have no idea why I did that in the painting of 9-18-2009.

Hesburgh Surprise at the Hidden Crucifix

In October of 2012, Linda said to me, "C'mon, get in the car, we are going for a ride. Of course, I gave her all kinds of grief. Like a lot of coaches, I like to follow a schedule and don't like surprises that take me off schedule.

"Just shut up and get in the car," she said.

We made a left out of our neighborhood up Notre Dame Avenue, a left turn at Holy Cross Drive past the security post near the Notre Dame Bookstore at the edge of campus and around the western edge of campus. I was riding shotgun and we were taking the route we normally took when we went to the Grotto.

"Where are we going?"

All of a sudden we made the left by the Grotto. We drove to the spot where we park when we are going to the Hidden Crucifix. After we parked, I looked down the path and I could see some people in a golf cart.

At first I thought it was my daughter Karen and her husband Jamie, who were in town at the time. But, then I could tell it was three people, Melanie, Father Austin Collins and Father Hesburgh.

As we walked down the path to the Hidden Crucifix I started to cry.

Melanie helped Father Hesburgh out of the golf cart.

As we reached the front of the Hidden

Crucifix, there was a new bench, located behind the kneeler directly in front of the Hidden Crucifix. Linda had worked the previous many months with the Congregation of Holy Cross brothers to have the bench installed.

There was a plaque on the bench that said,

In honor of one who has touched so many
Richard "Digger" Phelps
*   "The power of prayer is the will to win."*
With love, your devoted companion

Father Ted blessed the bench. I have never been so touched.

Even today when someone asks me about it I have a hard time putting it into words. To have Father Ted there to bless it meant everything.

That prayer is my favorite prayer, one I write on notes when I send people medals or when I just send an inspirational card.

Linda had another bench placed at the front of the Fatima Retreat House by St. Joseph Lake, because Linda and I always go over there and sit. So we went over and Father Ted blessed that one too.

For him to bless the bench at the Hidden Crucifix just added to the spirituality of it for me. It has to be the most meaningful and spiritually uplifting place on this campus for

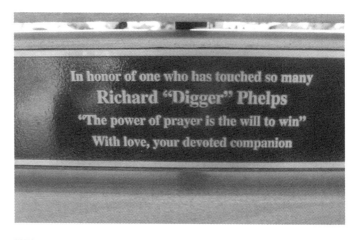

One of the greatest honors of my life was having Father Ted Bless this bench on October 12, 2012. I was joined by Father Austin Collins, my fiancē Linda, and Father Ted.

me. It is Sacred Turf.

It was a day and an experience I will never forget.

John Calipari

John Calipari brought his eighth-ranked Kentucky team to South Bend in November of 2012 to play the Irish in a regular season game. He had never been to Notre Dame so Linda and I wanted to show him the campus. Linda knew him from the days when she lived in Memphis and John was the coach at the University of Memphis. They had some mutual friends.

We took John to the Grotto, and he lit a candle for this mother. We then took him to the Hidden Crucifix. He took pictures at each place and was just enthralled by the campus, and its tradition and spirituality. John is a lifetime catholic who goes to Mass just about every day.

During the tour, I told him all about Father Hesburgh and what he had meant to the spirituality of this place, and his impact on Civil Rights in this country….and, his impact on my career as coach, and my life in general.

When I took him back to the downtown Doubletree Hotel, where they were staying, he said, "Digger, can we go back to the Grotto? I want to say the Rosary for my Mom."

I said, "No problem." So we went back to the Grotto and parked behind Corby Hall. I stayed in the car as he said the Rosary in solitude. I couldn't help but think of this scene. Here was the head basketball coach at Kentucky, saying a rosary at the Notre Dame Grotto.

What would Adolph Rupp have thought?

He said the Rosary and came back to the car and he said, "You know, it must be something coaching at a place like this."

I replied with a smile, "Why, you thinking about it?"

"That's a good way for you to finish your career." He just laughed.

John really enjoyed his visit to Notre Dame, although the Irish did beat his Wildcats the next night.

Later that season he called me a couple of times, and sent messages I appreciated. Some of them were as follows.

Cal said, "Digger — You know, it's crazy, I was thinking about you the other day when we were getting ready to play Kansas, because you would always be at those games. I miss you! I miss you!"

Later in the season, I got another:

Cal said, "Digger — You had better be at Mass, and not still sleeping at 8:50 a.m. I bet it's cold up here. I miss you man! I miss my man Digger! … lighting candles for my mom. Call me. Even if you want to come down for a couple of days and watch my team. 2-2-1 press. Talk to you."

Tuesdays with Digger

Every Tuesday I go to the campus, making stops at various places that are special to me. That obviously includes the Hidden Crucifix and the Grotto.

I light a lot of candles for people every week. I light one for Mike Brey's mother, who died in 2015 when the Irish won the ACC Championship and got to the Elite Eight. She died during the postseason that year and I know that had to be tough. Mike is a good friend and has really done a great job. He is a great fit for Notre Dame.

I light one for John Calipari's mother and it is next to the candle for Mike Brey's mom. Mike's dad died a year later. His candle is next to his wife. Mike knew I lit a candle for his mom and he told John on a recruiting trip that the candle for Mike's mom and John's mom are next to each other.

One year, Cal was in New York for Christmas week. He texted me a picture of St. Jude from St. Patrick's Cathedral. That's John Calipari.

I also light a candle for Tim Kempton's (starting Notre Dame center in 1980s) High School Coach, Ralph Willard. His son, Kevin Willard, now coaches at Seton Hall. Ralph has AFIB.

On Feb. 13, 2016, when Louisville was at

Notre Dame, I took Ralph to the grotto to light a candle for his dad. We then went to the Hidden Crucifix. Ralph is a big asset to Rick Pitino at Louisville.

There is also a candle for Steve Lavin's (former UCLA coach) dad at the Grotto. When he was the coach at St. John's I took him to the Grotto and he lit a candle for his dad. I have continued the tradition.

I told Father Hesburgh about my Tuesday routine. In many ways he is the inspiration for it because we talked so much about the spirituality of the campus and its traditions.

What has been incredible about the Tuesday experience is how fast it goes and how fast that next Tuesday comes back around. It takes me about 45 minutes overall. But it is timeless.

For whatever reason - whatever goes on during the week – and you think it drags, because, you've got this, you've got that. But, all of a sudden, the next thing I know, I can't believe it's Tuesday. I can't believe I'm headed to the Grotto to light the candles and to the Hidden Crucifix. It just seems like this whole spiritual experience is timeless, because it just happens with the snap of a finger versus a seven-day week.

I say my morning prayers over by Carroll Hall at the South end of campus. There is a Christmas tree near the building - a fir tree.

When I first came to Notre Dame, I noticed on one of my walks that the tree was cut in half, because back then in the early '70's, you could have a tree in your dorm.

Well, Carroll Hall didn't have it. Probably one of the other dorms stole the top of that tree - about six feet worth.

Over time the tree has grown back! It is now about 80-feet tall! I call it the "Miracle Christmas Tree at Carroll Hall". When I speak at Carroll Hall every fall in November, between fall break and Thanksgiving, we decorate that tree with about 15 bulbs every early December, so that it will help put that side of campus in the Christmas spirit.

Sharing A Miracle of the Hidden Cross

I get a lot of letters from people who know how much this campus means to me. Many of the letters are from people I have sent medals to as they try to find the strength to cope with a physical ailment or one of life's significant problems.

But one of the letters was sent to me as a complete surprise a couple of years ago. It contained a story from Beverley Mikesell and Diane Crawford who are from nearby Indiana cities of Mishawaka and Granger (respectively).

I am not going to summarize their story because I don't think I could do it justice.

Below is a copy of their letter to me.

*How does one start to share a miracle?
Our hope is that by sharing our wondrous
experience, we can bring others to believe and have
faith that God is there for each of us in what seems to
be our darkest hours of need. One must listen to His
calling, have faith, believe and remember that all is in
God's timing and not ours.*

*Before we begin to share our wondrous
experience, we feel it is necessary to give you some
family background regarding our religious beliefs
and our dad's health history. By doing this we
hope that you will have a better understanding of
our experience at the Hidden Cross, but most of all
believe that miracles can happen to and for anyone if
you believe and trust in God for them.*

*Our mom is Catholic and is strong in her faith.
She attends Mass every Sunday and practices the
beliefs of the church. Our dad was raised Protestant
attending a missionary church as a child.*

*When our parents married we were both baptized
Catholic. When we were small we practiced both
Catholic and Protestant ways. We did not go to
church on a regular basis, but religion was still an
important part of our life. We received teachings of
both religions and attended both the Catholic and
Missionary Church on occasions. Our parents agreed
that when we were old enough to decide, it would be
our choice.*

As adults we choose to make Holy Communion, and marry in the Catholic Church. Our dad too made his Holy Communion and remarried our mom in the Catholic Church on their 25th wedding anniversary. Our dad has a strong faith in God, prays to God and lives by God, but his philosophy is,"how you live your life outside the church and what you do to all mankind counts, not just what you do at church or with your church family."

Even though dad does not attend church regularly like our mom, he does pray and has a personal relationship with our Lord.

Our parents taught us about having the love of God in our hearts. Mom taught us the Catholic religion and answered any questions we had about anything. Dad taught us how to have a spiritual relationship with God. God is everywhere, you can pray to him anytime, anywhere, and he is listening to you. All of this gave us a strong foundation in our faith. This also gave us a loving home and a very tight bond with each other. We're family and we know love.

Our dad is 78-years-old. He is a good man with a determined mind. He always has the right answers if you have a problem. He will do anything for anyone. He is strong and still very hard working. If and when he does get sick, it has to be really severe before he will say anything about it.

Our first experience with dad's health was 12 years ago. He was having chest pains and our mom recognized the fact that he was not looking himself or acting like himself. Mom finally squeezed it out of him and too him to the ER. There they admitted dad for 24 hour observation and ended up with quadruple bypass heart surgery. He recovered rapidly with the love of his wife and family. He quit smoking at that time, but eight months later he started again.

Dad was doing well with no severe episodes or sickness until September of 2010. Dad started with cold symptoms that did not go away and gradually became worse. We all felt this could not be a cold, but dad was insistent that there was nothing wrong with him; this was a bad cold.

He refused to see his doctor. He began to develop a severe cough that kept getting worse and it was now affecting his daily life. Our mom at that time insisted that he see the doctor and have some tests done. She was not taking no for an answer.

Dad gave no fight, unknown to us he was coughing up blood and he now was ready to admit he needed help. Tests were done, a biopsy was taken and he was diagnosed on December 17, 2010 with Stage 3 Lung Cancer. The doctor who performed the biopsy told us dad had two tumors in his right lung.

Dad had been a smoker for 65 years and worked as a diesel mechanic and was constantly surrounded by gas and diesel fuel fumes for 40 years. Even with these conditions our first thoughts were the same as any family, why? How is mom going to handle this? Who are we going to turn to for help and guidance in finding the best care for him?

We were at a loss, felt numb, our hearts were heavy and aching, but we knew we had to be strong for dad with the obstacles ahead. Our parents needed us more than ever now. They always have been there for us; it was now our time to be there for them. We knew that we could not do this alone. God was our hope.

On December 19, 2010, in the evening, we knew we had to go to the grotto; light candles for our parents, and pray for strength and guidance. It was a dark, cold and icy night. We traveled carefully on the snow-covered roads where my sister and I met at the guard station at the entrance to the Notre Dame campus.

The campus was quiet since most of the students had gone home for Christmas break. We explained to the guard that we needed to get to the grotto and he seemed to understand with no questions asked. We parked one car at the Hammes Bookstore parking lot and drove the other car through the gate onto campus.

When we reached the Grotto, we were not sure where to park; we found a small parking area that was under construction north east of the Grotto. We were in the car putting on our warm gear and noticed bright lights behind us. We didn't see anything following us when we came in, but we never gave it much thought.

The sidewalks were very icy and snow covered

due to no student traffic. As we were walking down the sidewalk towards the Grotto, we suddenly heard someone behind us walking. We turned around and saw a gentleman. We turned to him to let him know we were aware of his presence and asked him if he would like to go ahead of us because we were walking slowly due to the icy conditions.

He politely refused and said to us, "Oh No! I'm on this journey with you; let's just take all this beauty together. I'll pray with you. We had no fear in our hearts, only peace, and really did not think much about what he said at the time.

We made our way down the path and stairs to the Grotto, lit our candles and prayed. We placed our hands on the stone from Lourdes and quietly said our prayer. The gentleman was on the other side of the Grotto lighting his candle and praying.

The nativity scene was lit and we proceeded to walk over to it. As we turned, the gentleman was standing at the corner of it. We made our way back to the Grotto and we were whispering that maybe the church would be open. We were hoping to find a priest to talk and pray with.

At that time, the gentleman touched our shoulders and said to us, "I know your hearts are troubled. I don't know why, but I do know that I need to lead you to a special place. Not everyone knows about this place, and it is the belief that one needs to find it on his or her own, but I need to lead you there now.

You need the Hidden Cross. Would you follow me there?

There was no fear; we immediately responded yes. We felt a sense of peace, love and trust. We thanked him and as we were walking back to our car, he started to explain the cross to us.

He told us that Digger Phelps visits the cross, and during his battle with cancer, he found peace there. He explained that the Cross was on the holiest grounds of all of Notre Dame. He then began to explain pictures that Digger Phelps had taken of the Cross and what had appeared in them.

A crown of thorns surrounded the cross. We took all of his words in. As we approached our car, the gentleman headed to a white pickup truck that was parked directly behind our car. We followed him.

He got out of his truck and started to walk into the wooded are. We continued to follow.

The snow and ice made it difficult, but it seemed effortless. We came upon a mound that held the most beautiful crosses we had ever seen. We knelt before it and prayed.

The gentleman prayed with us. We noticed what looked like snow covered steps and asked if it would be ok to walk up to the cross and he replied yes.

We carefully walked up the stairs and placed our hands on Jesus's feet and began to pray aloud. We could hear the gentleman pray with us.

As we finished our prayer, we stood facing the cross, looked at it, and thanked Jesus for hearing our prayers.

As we turned away, the gentleman was gone. Just as he appeared to us from nowhere, he disappeared the same. We wanted to thank him, but he was gone. At that time, we in our hearts knew that an angel was sent to us from God to help guide us.

When we got into our car, we felt such a sense of peace, love, calmness and serenity that we have never felt so strong before. A huge weight had been lifted off our hearts. We can't describe the peace and strength that was given to us that night.

As each of us arrived at our homes, we just had to call each other and talk about what had just happened. We both confirmed it had to be an angel sent to us in our darkest hours.

The next day, our dad had an appointment to see the oncologist for the first time. He was going to review his recent PET scan with us. As we talked with him about the report from the biopsy, we questioned him about the two tumors. The oncologist then stated to us that our dad only had one tumor and he was going to treat it very aggressively. Our dad was a strong man and he was very positive about the outcome.

At that moment my sister and I knew where we had to go after hearing this news. We went back to the Hidden Cross at Notre Dame and gave thanks to God for hearing our prayers.

After our visit at the Cross, we went to my

parents home and shared our experience with them. Dad had tears in his eyes. He knew God had listened to our prayers. Dad then told us that on the day that he found out he had cancer, he prayed to the "Big Man Upstairs" to help him quit smoking; he had tried several times before with no success.

Dad knew he had to this time. God answered his prayer. He quit smoking cold turkey. His last pack of cigarettes and lighter lay on the table beside him, untouched, as a reminder.

Every night we went to the Hidden Cross and thanked God for our answered prayers. For we knew that once we asked, they were answered. God's word says, "Therefore I say to you, whatever things you ask, when you pray, believe that you receive them, and you will have them." Mark 11:24.

We never saw our angel again, but we do feel the love and peace we found that night at the Hidden Cross at every visit. We know we are standing on Holy ground. We continue to go to the cross and pray for our mom and dad.

At this time our dad has overcome 31 of 35 radiation treatments and 13 chemo treatments with very few side effects. Radiation was the worst for him. We're not saying dad has no pain, he does, but God gave him the strength and stamina to get through it.

The doctor was impressed that our dad endured 31 treatments of radiation. Not many people can tolerate that many. Our dad had weight loss, but not as severe as expected. He did lose his hair, but not till the very end of treatment, and it is already growing back.

The tumor shrunk from a large walnut side to the size of a marble. The tumor is nothing but scar tissue at this time.

The cancer is gone and dad is getting stronger each day. Our mom has been strong for dad as always. Dad had put her through a rough time, but God gave her the strength to get through this. And dad continues to pray for himself and his new friends that are stricken with this disease.

He shares his story hoping to give others strength to overcome their own personal battles. And dad has been smoke free since the beginning of his journey to healing.

There truly is something special about the Hidden Cross. We will never be able to thank our angel enough for sharing it with us that night.

"For where two or three are gathered together in my name, I am there in the midst of them."

The song "Standing on Holy Ground," written by Geron Davis truly describes this wondrous place we have come to know as the Hidden Cross.

Verse 1
   When I walked through the doors,
   I sensed his presence
   And I knew this was a place where love abounds
   For this is a temple

The God we love abides here,
And we are standing in His presence on holy
ground.

Chorus
We are standing on holy ground
And I know that there are angels all around.
Let us praise Jesus now,
We are standing in his presence on holy ground.

Verse 2
In his presence I know there is
Joy beyond all measure,
And at His feet,
Sweet peace of mind can still be found.
For when we have a need,
He is still the answer,
Reach out and claim it
For we are standing on holy ground

I communicated with their dad as he went through his physical challenges and I hope I gave him hope and inspiration. On January 30, 2016, I received this message from Diana.

"Just wanted you to know that we are at the Hidden Cross with my sweet Dad today. His last visit. He does not have much time left. He put up a good fight. Blessed to have him these five years, he wanted to visit his favorite place to pray. God gave him the strength today to come."

Beverley Mikesell and Diane Crawford had quite a story to tell about the Hidden Crucifix.

I had given Diane medals for Elton and he had them until the day he died, March 20, 2016, which was fittingly Palm Sunday. He had been given two years to live when they first went to the Hidden Crucifix. He lived for five.

ND Grads in the Priesthood ... The Hesburgh Effect

What is amazing today is that a lot of the C.S.C. priests at Notre Dame were students when I started here in the early 1970s. Current President Father John Jenkins was a student back then and so was Father Austin Collins, who was very close to Father Hesburgh. Father

Edward Malloy, who was also President of Notre Dame, was a student and a basketball player as an undergraduate.

Father Paul Doyle, a former football game priest, would stand on our 35 yard line, and start waving his arms up and down to the student section to get them fired up. I called him the "Black Swan."

It tells you something about the spiritual environment that we had on campus.

At times when I am with them I like to kid them and ask, "Do you guys realize that's a Lady on the Dome up there? Remember, it's the Blessed Mother." I have known them a long time and can throw them a shot and get away with it.

Actually, I had my own impact on a future priest when I was the head basketball coach at St. Gabriel's in Hazeltine, Pennsylvania. My student manager in 1965 was a kid named Tom O'Hara. When I came to Notre Dame in 1971, I ran into him at Moreau Seminary.

"What are you doing here?" I said. He was at Notre Dame studying to become a priest.

He became a C.S.C. priest and spent some time in Africa before becoming President of Kings College in Wilkes Barre, Penn., a Notre Dame sister school.

Four years ago, he was elected University Provincial at Notre Dame.

His first year in that position, I brought him the game ball from our state championship victory when he was manager of the St. Gabe's team. I gave it to him and said, "Here, this will inspire you to get the job done with C.S.Cs around here. "

It gives me great pride to see him here in that position.

The Hidden Crucifix in 1941

I always wondered how long the Hidden Crucifix has been at Notre Dame. I still don't know the answer, but I know it at least goes back to 1941, the year I was born. My co-author, Tim Bourret, is a second generation Domer. His dad, Chuck Bourret, was a Notre Dame engineering graduate in 1948.

But, Chuck came to Notre Dame as a freshman in 1941. It took him seven years to graduate because he spent three years in the U.S. Army in WWII.

Chuck enjoyed photography, and one perfect November fall afternoon as a freshman, he walked around campus taking pictures. He took some of the grotto, the church, the lake….and of the Hidden Crucifix.

Tim was going through his dad's personal pictures after he passed in 2013 and he came across these pictures. There was one picture of the Hidden Crucifix. It was dated on the back November 9, 1941, just five months after I was born.

Tim Bourret's dad took this picture of the Hidden Crucifix in 1941 when he was a freshman.

CHAPTER 8
THE MEDALS

The Game Medals

When I interviewed for the Notre Dame Head Basketball coaching position with Father Joyce at the Detroit Airport in April of 1971, we talked about what was expected of the Notre Dame coach in detail. The most important points were to graduate my players, don't get in trouble with the NCAA and to be competitive, which meant win 18 games a year (in an era with just 26 regular season games).

Late in the conversation, he said to me, "By the way, we also have a team Mass the day of the game." I said, "We had it at Fordham."

Father Joyce continued, "And, there will be a priest with you, even on the road, to say Mass. And, we also have game medals, not to pray to win, but to pray to do our best."

Father Joyce also made a point to say that the priest would sit on the bench, and wear a Roman Collar home and away. He believed that everyone needed to get ready for these games physically, mentally, and spiritually.

Many players would save the medals, or give them to family or friends. Bill Hanzlik, who played for me from 1976-80 before going on to a long NBA career as a player and coach, gave them to his mother and each year she made a bracelet from the collection of medals from each game.

In 1971-72, my first year, we were bad,

there is just no other way to say it. Johnny Dee's last team featured Austin Carr, Notre Dame's greatest player and still all-time leading scorer, and six other seniors who had played together for four years, including their year on the freshman team (freshmen were ineligible for the varsity in those days). But they had all graduated by the time I arrived on campus.

We finished 6-20 that first season and on the way to that record we suffered some of the worst losses in Notre Dame history. One of those came in Bloomington, Indiana where we lost to a 10th ranked Indiana team coached by my friend Bob Knight, 94-29. That's right, I didn't transpose the digits for our score, we lost by 65 in that game played a week before Christmas, still the worst margin of defeat in Notre Dame history.

Coach Knight is still a close friend, and we had spent a lot of time together prior to that game when he was at West Point and I was an assistant coach at Pennsylvania. We had attended a lot of the same clinics, and played golf together at West Point. But we were both in our first year at our respective programs and wanted to make an impression.

Father Jim Schultz was our game priest that night in Bloomington, which was the Dedication Game for Assembly Hall. On the bus ride home he said to me, "I want to be the game priest in two years when we come back here."

If he had to suffer through this game, and wanted to come back, he deserved it. "You got it Father."

Two years later, in December of 1973, we had John Shumate and Gary Brokaw, future NBA players in their second year as starters, and a freshman class that featured future Hall of Fame player Adrian Dantley. All three would be first-round NBA draft choices. Brokaw had sprained his ankle and could not play in this game, but we still beat an Indiana team that had gone to the Final Four the previous March, 73-67.

That was a huge win for our program over a third-ranked Indiana team, and that was a joyous bus ride back to South Bend. Father Schultz might have been the happiest.

Father Schultz continued to serve as a game priest on occasion during the 1970s and early 1980s. But, he became ill in 1982 and passed away. He is buried in the Holy Cross Community Cemetery on campus, the same place Father Hesburgh is buried.

About a week after the funeral, my secretary, Dottie Van Paris, came into my office and said, "Father Jim Schultz's brother is here to see you." Father Schultz had grown up in nearby Chesterton, Indiana and had family in the area, so I was not surprised by his visit.

He came into the office carrying a box of

medals Father Jim had saved from the games he had been the game priest. They had been blessed for all the game day Masses.

I appreciated the gesture by Father Jim's brother and I knew immediately I could put them to good use.

On a regular basis I received correspondence from Notre Dame fans, people from all over the world, who were sick or knew someone who was sick. I sent them an encouraging note, and now, started sending along the medals, telling them it had been blessed by a Notre Dame priest for one of our game day Masses.

There were a lot of medals in that box and it took until about the year 2000 before I started running out.

It was time to replenish the supply, so I decided I wanted to get two of my favorite and most meaningful medals. The first was the St. Jude medal, because that was always our game medal when we played at UCLA. The St. Jude medal is for hopeless causes. That was our feeling in the beginning of my career at Notre Dame when we were playing John Wooden's teams that had won so many championships and were the dominant force of college basketball.

By my third year we ended their 88-game winning streak and between 1976-77 and 1979-80 we beat them four straight years in Pawley

Pavilion, the first program to do that. Hanzlik, who as I said previously saved all his game medals for his mom, and Rich Branning, a native of California, were seniors who were on all four of those teams.

I also got medals with "The Lady on the Dome" on one side and Sacred Heart on the back.

So I took all these medals to Father Hesburgh and said, "Father, I give these medals to the sick, or people with problems, and I would like you to bless them so I can continue to give people some hope and continue this tradition. He did as I had asked in my presence, and I (as you will see later in this chapter), still send medals today.

I give them to the people with my prayer, "The power of prayer is the will to win." I tell them to keep the medals because they were blessed by Father Hesburgh.

The whole experience with these people has left an impact on me. It has given me personal spiritual fulfillment. It is one of the reasons I have lived in South Bend close to the Notre Dame campus and this Sacred Turf all these years.

Medal Stories

Mrs. Valvano

I roomed with Jim Valvano's brother, Nick, when I was at Rider, and got to know the family because they used to come to the Rider campus. I used to roughhouse with Bob Valvano, Jim's brother, in the Valvano car when we were kids.

Mrs. Valvano would come to campus to see Nick and bring us Italian food all the time, so I got on her good side. She was a great woman.

In 1983, we played in Raleigh, the year NC State won the NCAA Championship with the magic run that ended with a one-point victory over Houston. We beat NC State in Raleigh that year, 43-42 and I gave Mrs. Valvano a medal before that game. She showed Jim the medal before the game and he said, "Are you rooting for Digger and Notre Dame tonight mom?" He believed that's why we won.

Sarah Wright

Sarah Wright was a firm believer in the power of prayer and the medals that were blessed by Father Hesburgh. Below is a letter she sent me through John Markovich, who was our Head Athletic Trainer my first two years at Notre Dame.

Dear Coach,

I am writing in regards to support for the canonization of Father Ted Hesburgh. Last October, our son Ayden, was diagnosed with liver cancer. Prior to his diagnosis, he was a healthy sports loving, outdoor hunting 12-year-old.

At his diagnosis, the doctor informed me he had about three months to live. This of course was devastating to all of us.

He began chemotherapy immediately. While in the hospital, a good friend of the family, John Markovich, had been visiting a friend of his at Notre Dame, Digger Phelps.

Upon returning home, John brought some Notre Dame memorabilia to Ayden.

However, one piece stood out. It was the Miraculous Mary Medal.

Along with it was a card that informed us that Father Theodore Hesburgh said we needed to say a prayer each time we held this relic.

From that moment on, Ayden has had that charm hanging either on him personally, or his IV pole while in the hospital, or hanging over him as he slept at home at night.

It was during one of his hospital visits that Ayden awoke in a panic. He couldn't breathe, was white as a ghost, and was shaking uncontrollably.

After many attempts trying to figure out what was wrong, he finally told us he had had a dream. In this dream two hands came down to him and wrapped him in a white robe. He truly thought it was God coming down to take him to Heaven.

However, he was so overcome with emotion, that all he could do was cry! After many hours of comforting him, he realized it was God telling him everything was going to be OK.

Looking back at this, we realized that it was during this dream, that Ayden was wearing the Miraculous Mary Medal around his neck.

Fast forward eight months….Ayden is still here!!!

However, he is now getting ready to go into surgery to try and remove the tumors. Mind you, this wasn't even an option in the beginning.

However, we believe the power of prayer has gotten us where we are!

Prior to going into surgery, Ayden asked that the Miraculous Mary Medal be taken into the surgery room with him. The surgery took about five hours, but was successful. The surgeons told us that if they saw any more tumors while doing a scope before opening him up, they would not have proceeded with the surgery.

After doing the scope, they said they did not see any new tumors, so they proceeded.

However, after removing a couple of tumors, they found a few new spots that they did not see, nor did they show up on the scans prior to the surgery.

Since he was already opened up, they decided to go ahead and remove the ones they could.

After surgery, we told Ayden the results, and they had found a few other spots that they didn't know he originally had. He looked at us and said, "I knew they were going to find other spots.

I said, "How?"

He then said, God came to me last night (the night before the surgery) and told me they would find a few more spots, but everything was going to be OK!"

Please remember that the blessed Miraculous Mary Medal had not left his side.

It is now going on one year since the original diagnosis. He has had four rounds of Chemo since the surgery to try and kill off any cancer they did not see. We do scans on November 30th.

We truly believe that they will come back clean. From being told you have three months with your son, to him being with us a year later is truly a miracle in itself.

However, we feel that the blessed Miraculous Mary Medal was the door that allowed the two visits from God.

We believe that medal has truly helped our son.

Molly Walsh

I traveled to Westminster College near St. Louis, Missouri in 2008 to give a talk on leadership. During my time there, one of their students, Molly Walsh, gave me a tour of the campus.

Molly was interested in the subject of my speech, but she was more interested in talking about Notre Dame and her Catholic faith. An Irish Catholic, she followed Notre Dame sports, but had never been to Notre Dame and wanted to know about the Grotto and the religious environment.

We had a great talk while she gave me that tour.

I didn't hear from her again until the fall of 2010. She had graduated and was starting her career when she was taken to the hospital with pancreatitis. She reacted to some of the medicine they had given her and had a heart attack. What a challenge for a 22-year-old just a year out of college getting ready to start a career.

We talked to her for this book in the summer of 2016. I will let her tell the rest of the story.

"While I was in the hospital, I got Digger Phelps's book, *An Undertaker's Son*. I loved the stories and it made me want to visit Notre Dame all the more.

"So I wrote Coach Phelps a hand written letter from my hospital room and sent it to his home in Indiana.

"Soon after, he called me in the hospital. We talked about a lot of the chapters in the book, but I remember asking him about the Hidden Crucifix.

"I just thought that was so interesting to have that in the middle of campus and I told him I hoped to come to Notre Dame one day and he could show it to me.

"Digger wanted to do something for me in the interim, so he sent me two of the Hesburgh medals, St. Jude and Mary on the Dome.

"A lot of people come to Notre Dame for the first time for a football game. I came for Holy Week of 2011, just a few months after I got out of the hospital. Digger and Linda gave me the grand tour.

"I was overwhelmed. I still remember seeing the Grotto for the first time and then we went to the Hidden Crucifix. What an experience. Notre Dame is sacred turf!

"I have been back to Notre Dame three times since and I am doing well health wise.

"By the way, I still keep those medals with me everywhere I go. When I change pocket books, they are the first items I move."

Today, Molly is a fund raiser for a Catholic High School near St. Louis.

Officer Joe O'Sullivan

Joe O'Sullivan retired from the New York City Police Department in 2016. He and his brother-in-law came out to Notre Dame for the Brigham Young football game the weekend of October 20, 2012. Joe worked with a mutual friend of mine who worked in the NYPD, and he asked if I would give Joe and some members of his family a tour of Notre Dame the Saturday morning before the game.

I gave the complete Digger Tour, and that included a trip to the Grotto followed by a visit to the Hidden Crucifix. I told them the story of the Hidden Crucifix and how I had found out I had cancer while I was saying some prayers at that very spot in 2010.

All of a sudden, Joe began to cry. He was overcome with emotion because his nephew, who was just a couple of days old, was struggling to survive in a hospital in New York. The young boy, Colin McGrory, had some ailment that caused him to have labored breathing. The doctors were at a loss as to what was causing the issue.

Joe said some prayers at the Hidden Crucifix and we finished the tour.

The same day, I went home and brought him two medals and told him that Father Hesburgh had blessed them. "Bring them to Colin," I told him.

Joe flew back to New York on Sunday and met his mother, who brought the medals to the hospital and gave them to Joe's sister Kristen, Colin's mother. She brought them to the hospital.

Two days after they put the medals over Colin's bed, he began to breathe easier and he was at home by the end of the week.

Colin turned a healthy four years old in 2016.

Kristen asked Joe if I needed to get the medals back. I laughed and said those should stay with Colin the rest of his life. Those are his Hesburgh medals.

Ellie Faithful

The Monday after my co-author, Tim Bourret, wrote this chapter, he texted Clemson Head Golf Coach Larry Penley about his schedule for the coming season. In the reply, Coach Penley said he was at a hospital in nearby Greenville, South Carolina because his seven-month old grand-daughter, Ellie Faithful, was having trouble breathing.

"They have tried everything," Penley texted.

Having just interviewed Joe O'Sullivan about the story of his nephew, Bourret replied to Penley, a non-Catholic, that he needed a Hesburgh medal.

I had given Tim a Hesburgh medal many years ago when we started writing our book, *Digger Phelps's Tales from the Notre Dame Hardwood.*

Tim always carried the Mary on the Dome medal with him. So, at the end of work that day, he printed out the story on Joe O'Sullivan's nephew and brought his Hesburgh medal to the hospital in Greenville.

Penley and his family were glad to see Tim and he had Larry's wife, Heidi, read the O'Sullivan story right away in Ellie's hospital room.

Tim then taped the medal to the top of Ellie's bed and told them about the medals and Father Hesburgh.

A day later, Tim got a text from Coach Penley. Ellie had made an incredible improvement and was going to get out of the hospital the next day.

The two stories continued their similarities right to the end. Two days after Colin McGrory had received his Hesburgh medal, he left the hospital. Now it was just two days after Ellie Faithful received her medal that she was leaving the hospital.

"The power of prayer is the will to win."

CHAPTER 9
THE HESBURGH STAMP

In conjunction with the 1984 Olympics in Los Angeles, the United States Postal Service announced four stamps with the Olympic theme. One was about basketball.

In the summer of 1983, at a national AAU Tournament at Notre Dame, the basketball stamp was unveiled at a luncheon.

I was at the luncheon and sat next to a person from the Postal Service. I told him that as a second grader we used to receive a publication called the "Weekly Reader." Many times it had an article that talked about the new stamps that had just been published.

So, as a second grader, I read about the new stamps and would then go to the post office and buy the stamp for three cents. I then came home, went to my room and put them in a stamp album.

The guy said to me, "You were a stamp collector?" I said, "Yes, back to the second grade."

He asked me if I still collected them and I said yes. I collected Duck stamps because they had value.

So, the person said to me, "You should be on the committee. "

I said, "What committee?"

He said, "The Citizens Stamp Advisory Committee. They are the people who recommend the stamp subjects to the

Postmaster General."

I told him immediately that I was interested.

So that December of 1983 I went to a meeting in Washington, D.C. that was conducted by the US Postal Service and that next year, I was named to the committee. It was in the middle of my career as Notre Dame basketball coach, but the meetings were quarterly and I was able to plan in advance.

People from all over the United States sent in recommendations for new stamps. The committee received thousands of letters with recommendations in a year.

The recommendations were put into categories and we met and discussed them at meetings mostly held in Washington, D.C.

About 50 stamps were published each year and a lot of work went into the background research. Many of the stamps were published in coordination with anniversaries. The Hesburgh stamp is an example, as it will be published in 2017, the same year as his 100th birthday.

Politicians don't make decisions on stamps. They make requests just like anyone else. A U.S. President and the Postmaster General can recommend a stamp to the Citizen Stamp Advisory Committee. The committee reviews it and then makes their recommendations to the Postmaster General, who makes the final decision.

The committee is made up of people from different areas of the country and different lifestyles and that is one of the reasons it really is the *Citizens* Stamp Advisory Committee.

I stayed on the committee until 2006. It was a great 22 years and I had the opportunity to meet some very interesting people. One of the people with me on the committee for much of my time was the well known actor Carl Mauldin.

By 1988, I was the chairman of the sports subcommittee. I was part of some great projects that dealt with sports, but the most rewarding was the Rockne Stamp.

Knute Rockne's 100th birthday was on March 4, 1988, so leading up to that week we discussed having a Rockne stamp. That discussion began in 1986. That is how far you have to plan in advance when you have a specific date of issue in mind.

Most stamps have a ceremony to commemorate the first day of issue and I thought it only made sense to have the Rockne Stamp ceremony at Notre Dame.

In early 1987 we played Maryland in Cole Fieldhouse. John Simpson was the director of the Secret Service and is a good friend. I asked him if we could give our team a tour of the West Wing of the White House. President Ronald Reagan was going to be out of town in

California. I wanted the team to see the Oval Office.

Simpson and I were walking around the White House during the tour. I asked him, "How can I get President Reagan to come out for the first day of issue celebration for the Rockne Stamp next year?" It was already scheduled for March 9, 1988.

I wanted him to come out because he was the Gipper in the film *Knute Rockne All-American* and I knew he would be a huge hit and bring attention to the ceremony like no other. He had been to Notre Dame many times before, including as graduation speaker in 1980 just after he had been elected President.

John said to me, "Just come to the White House and ask him."

I said, "You want me to just come up and knock on the front door?"

He laughed and said, "Make an appointment to come see him."

So the following May I flew to Washington, D.C. to meet with President Reagan in the Oval Office. Simpson was with me for that meeting.

President Reagan was fully supportive of the idea and it was put on his calendar a full 10 months ahead of the ceremony. As the date of the event got closer, I just prayed there would not be some world crisis that would force his cancellation.

The Rockne Stamp Ceremony

During breakfast, before the Rockne Ceremony, postmaster Tony Frank, Dickie Rustin (who also worked for the Postal Service) and I talked about having over 12,000 people at the ceremony. This was Tony Frank's first ceremony as Postmaster General. Frank said to Rustin, "Are all ceremonies like this?" Rustin laughed and said "No".

The Postal Service began a series of stamps in the 1980s called the American Sports Series. The Rockne stamp (then 22 cents) was the sixth in the series and followed stamps issued for Babe Zaharias, Bobby Jones, Babe Ruth, Jim Thorpe and Roberto Clemente. It was just the third stamp that dealt with football.

During the First Day Issue Celebration at the Joyce ACC (now known as the Purcell Pavilion) we had a stage. The Notre Dame football team sat in front of the stage. Tim Brown had just won the Heisman Trophy the previous fall and he was with the team.

At one point in the event Brown left his seat, went in front of the stage and caught a pass from President Reagan. Video of that pass made the national news that night.

To this day when I see Tim Brown I tell him, "Forget the Heisman Trophy, the only pass you caught that meant anything was the one you caught from the Gipper (President Reagan) the day we dedicated the Rockne Stamp."

The Purcell Pavilion held 11,343 seats back then and there were another 1,000 on the floor. It was packed.

The speakers included Father Edward Malloy, the Notre Dame President at the time, and Postmaster General Frank.

Then of course President Reagan gave the keynote speech. Below is one of President Reagan's comments that day.

"I would like to interject here, if I could, that it's difficult to stand before you and make you understand how great that legend was at that time. It isn't just a memory here and of those who knew him, but throughout this nation he was a living legend. Millions of Americans just automatically rooted for him on Saturday afternoon and rooted, therefore, for Notre Dame.

"Now, of course, the Rockne legend stood for fair play and honor, but you know, it was thoroughly American in another way. It was practical. It placed a value on devastating quickness and agility and on confounding the opposition with good old American cleverness.

"But most of all, the Rockne legend meant this -- when you think about it, it's what's been taught here at Notre Dame since her founding: that on or off the field, it is faith that makes the difference, it is faith that makes great things happen."

The Postal Service sells the stamps at all the first day issue ceremonies. They really had no idea how strong the interest would be. The stamp was so popular they eventually ran out.

Booing the Postmaster General

During one of our stamp committee meetings, I recommended we do a stamp in conjunction with the 100-year anniversary of basketball (1991). It was approved and we had the celebration in Springfield, Massachusetts where the sport was invented.

We had the celebration during half time of an exhibition game Notre Dame played against the Soviet Union. The game was sold out and over 8,000 people were expected. I was on the court for the halftime ceremony and introduced Postmaster Tony Frank.

This game was played in January and the month before, the Postal Service had approved a three-cent increase to the price of a stamp. That was still fresh on the minds of the fans in attendance. So when I introduced Tony, the crowd booed.

I felt bad for Tony because he was not the one that made the decision. The Board of Postal Governors made it. As he came up to the podium to speak, I tried to lighten the mood and said to him with a smile on my face, "A little different than the reception at Notre Dame?"

Father Hesburgh will have a "Forever Stamp" in his honor in conjunction with his 100th birthday in 2017. The first-day issue will be on September 1st on the Notre Dame campus.

Hesburgh Stamp Approval

Because of my relationship with Father Hesburgh over the years, it was my mission to get him a stamp. On March 4, 2015 there was a reception at the Morris Inn immediately following his funeral.

At the reception I saw Father John Jenkins, Notre Dame's current President, and Father Dick Warner, a retired CSC priest who was here from Rome for the funeral. I told them that I would work on getting Fr. Hesburgh a Forever Stamp.

I had never discussed with Fr. Ted my intentions to request a Forever Stamp in his honor when he was alive. Stamps are only created to honor a person after they are deceased.

Jerry Hammes, a university benefactor, wrote me and asked if there was a way to get Fr. Hesburgh a stamp while he was alive. I actually sent a letter requesting it, but the Board of Governors was not willing to change their policy. To this day no living person has received a stamp.

Soon after the funeral, I contacted the Postal Service and followed the process to get information to the committee about Father Hesburgh to see if we could get him a Forever Stamp. With 22 years of experience on the committee, I knew the process and knew what the committee was looking for in terms of information that would support our campaign for a Fr. Hesburgh stamp.

All our hard work and our hopes became a reality on Tuesday, September 20, 2016 when it was announced that the Postal Service would issue a Forever Stamp of Father Hesburgh. As you can see by the picture of the stamp in this chapter, it is a rendering of Hesburgh on the Notre Dame campus with the Golden Dome in the background.

The announcement of new stamps for 2017 also included one for President John F. Kennedy, who was himself born in 1917.

The first day of issue for the Father Hesburgh Forever Stamp will be September 1, 2017 and the ceremony will be at the Purcell Pavilion. It will be on the Friday before Notre Dame's 2017 home opening football game against Temple University.

The First Day of Issue Ceremony requires significant, long term planning. Because of my experience with the Citizens Stamp Advisory Committee, especially with the Rockne Stamp Ceremony, I was honored to work with the Postal Service team on the planning of this special event. Paul Browne is the VP of Public Affairs and Communications for Notre Dame.

On behalf of Fr. John, Paul has been the leader at Notre Dame working with me on this event. At my suggestion Fr. Jenkins and Paul invited Condoleezza Rice to be the key note speaker.

Paul texted me on July 9, 2016, the night of a surprise birthday party Linda organized for me at the ACC. The text said, "Happy Birthday!"

The text then said, "Condi said yes."

That was all pending the confirmation of the stamp of course, which came two months later. But we asked her ahead of time because we knew she had a full calendar.

As we have said earlier in this book, Father Hesburgh had great respect for Rice and we thought she would be someone who could convey the true spirit of what Father Ted meant to Notre Dame and to the world.

Rice grew up in Alabama and went to undergraduate school at the University of Denver. Father Ted knew her father and personally recruited her to come to Notre Dame to get her Masters degree. Notre Dame had become coed and with the Civil Rights act recently passed, he wanted to recruit African American women to Notre Dame.

Father Ted followed her journey and he was very proud of what she did with George H.W. Bush in the National Security Office. Then she worked as Secretary of State for four years under George W. Bush. She spent 12 years in the White House.

When she spoke at the Hesburgh Memorial Service, I said to myself, "She has to be the speaker at the first day issue ceremony." Her entertaining story that night told of the subtle ways Hesburgh motivated her in her efforts as National Security Advisor to forge peace between the Palestinians and the Israelis:

"When I was National Security Advisor, he called me a few days after September 11 — those were horrible days — just to offer prayer. And when I was Secretary of State, he would call once in a while. He called one day. I had just returned from one of my 24 trips to Israel and the Palestinian territories to try to forge peace between Palestinians and Israelis, and he said, 'You sound tired.' (laughter)

"Of course I was tired, but I wasn't about to tell Father Ted that I was tired. He said, 'I know the work is hard, but it has to be done.'

"And then he made an offer. He said, 'Why don't you bring the Israeli prime minister and the Palestinian Authority President to our retreat, the Notre Dame retreat in Wisconsin, and get them away from Washington.'

"Now, I have to admit, my mind was spinning at the thought of telling the prime minister of Israel and the Palestinian Authority president that they ought to come to Catholic Notre Dame to discuss peace. (laughter)

"I would have loved to have done it! I never

quite got them that far, but somehow I was encouraged and spurred ahead to try because Father Hesburgh understood that you can never accept the world as it is. You have to work for the world as it should be. "

We had a meeting at Notre Dame with about 25 people on September 23, 2016 . At that point everyone was given their job description for the ceremony.

The meeting included people from campus safety, Notre Dame public relations, the Notre Dame Alumni Association, University administrators and the athletic department.

Father Austin Collins was there as well and will be responsible for inviting the Notre Dame priests, brothers and nuns, especially those close to Hesburgh, to come to the ceremony.

The ceremony will include a video on Father Ted's life. Father Jenkins will speak representing Notre Dame, and the Postmaster General is scheduled to speak. Then, along with Father Jenkins, the Postmaster General will unveil the stamp. Following the unveiling, Rice will speak about how Father Ted touched her life. Provincial Father Tom O'Hara will give the final blessing.

To honor Father Hesburgh with a Forever Stamp, has been very rewarding for me personally. The impact he has had on my life has been significant during my career at

Notre Dame as a coach and after Notre Dame, coaching the streets.

What he did with The Civil Rights Act starting in 1957, was very important to this country and the world. It started with African Americans, but since then all races and religions have been positively affected by the Civil Rights Act.

That is the main reason I believed he should have this stamp. But, also with a world-record 150 honorary degrees, it shows the level of respect schools from all over the world had for him and the effect he had on education.

He is one of the most important Americans of the last 100 years.

March 4, 2015, Father Ted was laid to rest, but his spirit within my soul will never be buried.
(Photo by Barbara Johnson, University of Notre Dame Multimedia Services.

APPENDIX
HESBURGH HONORARY DEGREES

*Father Hesburgh's Record Breaking 150
Honorary Degrees*

It is internationally recognized that Father Hesburgh owns the world record for honorary degrees with 150. Here are some facts about the list, followed by a chronological listing by school.

• The time span of the conferring of degrees took place over 48 years.
• Seven of the eight Ivy League schools (all but Cornell) honored Hesburgh with an honorary degree.
• The University of San Diego in California was the only school to honor Hesburgh twice.
• Le Moyne College in Syracuse, New York, was the first institution to present Hesburgh with an honorary degree in 1954, just two years after he had become president at Notre Dame. Le Moyne is located in Syracuse, N.Y., Hesburgh's hometown.
• Hesburgh did not get an honorary degree from Notre Dame until 1984. It was his 101st honorary degree.
• Hesburgh received at least one honorary degree every year between 1965 and 2002, a streak of 38 consecutive years.
• The only years Hesburgh did not receive an honorary degree between 1954-2002 were 1957,

1959 and 1964. We suspect he was a little busy during the spring of 1964 as that was the time the Civil Rights Amendment was wrapped up.

• The most honorary degrees Hesburgh received in one year was 1981 when he received nine.

• He earned 50 of the 150 in the decade of the 1980s, including 39 between 1980-85.

• Hesburgh received honorary degrees from schools in 35 different states, plus Washington, D.C (3). New York (16), Pennsylvania (15) and Indiana (14) were the states he visited the most to receive the degrees.

• Hesburgh received honorary degrees from institutions in 15 countries outside of the United States.

• The 150th and final degree Hesburgh received was from the University of San Diego in 2002.

Father Hesburgh's 150 Honorary Degrees

1954–59
• Le Moyne College, Syracuse, New York, 1954
• Bradley University, Peoria, Illinois, 1955
• Catholic University of Santiago, Chile, 1956
• St. Benedict's College, Kansas, 1958
• Villanova University, Villanova, Pennsylvania, 1958
• Dartmouth College, Hanover, New Hampshire, 1958

1960–69

- University of Rhode Island, Kingston, Rhode Island, 1960
- Columbia University, New York, New York, 1961
- Princeton University, Princeton, New Jersey, 1961
- Brandeis University, Waltham, Massachusetts, 1962
- Indiana University, Bloomington, Indiana, 1962
- Northwestern University, Evanston, Illinois, 1963
- Lafayette College, Easton, Pennsylvania, 1963
- Honorary Citizen, University of Vienna, Austria, 1965
- University of California, Los Angeles, California, 1965
- St. Louis University, Baguio City, Philippines, 1965
- Gonzaga University, Spokane, Washington, 1965
- Temple University, Philadelphia, Pennsylvania, 1965
- University of Montreal, Canada, 1965
- University of Illinois, Urbana, Illinois, 1966
- Atlanta University, Atlanta, Georgia, 1966
- Wabash College, Crawfordsville, Indiana, 1966
- Fordham University, Bronx, New York, 1967
- Manchester College, North Manchester,

Indiana, 1967
- Valparaiso University, Valparaiso, Indiana, 1967
- Providence College, Providence, Rhode Island, 1968
- University of Southern California, Los Angeles, 1968
- Michigan State University, East Lansing, Michigan, 1968
- Saint Mary's College, Notre Dame, Indiana, 1969
- Saint Louis University, Saint Louis, Missouri, 1969
- Catholic University of America, Washington, D.C., 1969

1970–79
- Loyola University, Chicago, Illinois, 1970
- Anderson College, Anderson, Indiana, 1970
- State University of New York, Albany, New York, 1970
- Utah State University, Logan, Utah, 1971
- Lehigh University, Bethlehem, Pennsylvania, 1971
- Yale University, New Haven, Connecticut, 1971
- King's College, Wilkes-Barre, Pennsylvania, 1972
- Stonehill College, North Easton, Massachusetts, 1972

- Alma College, Alma, Michigan, 1972
- Syracuse University, Syracuse, New York, 1973
- Marymount College, Tarrytown, New York, 1973
- Hobart and William Smith Colleges, Geneva, New York, 1973
- Hebrew Union College, Cincinnati, Ohio, 1973
- Harvard University, Cambridge, Massachusetts, 1973
- Regis College, Denver, Colorado, 1974
- Lincoln University, Lincoln University, Pennsylvania, 1974
- Tufts University, Medford, Massachusetts, 1974
- The University of the South, Sewanee, Tennessee, 1974
- University of Portland, Portland, Oregon, 1975
- Fairfield University, Fairfield, Connecticut, 1975
- Davidson College, Davidson, North Carolina, 1976
- College of New Rochelle, New Rochelle, New York, 1976
- University of Denver, Denver, Colorado, 1976
- Beloit College, Beloit, Wisconsin, 1976
- Dickinson College, Carlisle, Pennsylvania, 1977
- Georgetown University, Washington, D.C., 1977
- Queens College, Flushing, New York, 1977

- Laval University, Quebec, Canada, 1977
- Katholieke Universiteit Leuven, Leuven, Belgium, February 1978
- University of South Carolina, Columbia, South Carolina, 1978
- University of Pennsylvania, Philadelphia, Pennsylvania, 1978
- Universite' Catholique de Louvain, Louvain-la-Neuve, Belgium, 1978
- Duquesne University, Pittsburgh, Pennsylvania, 1978
- St. Francis Xavier University, Antigonish, Nova Scotia, 1978
- University of Evansville, Evansville, Indiana, 1979
- Albion College, Albion, Michigan, 1979
- University of Utah, Salt Lake City, Utah, 1979
- Assumption College, Worcester, Massachusetts, 1979

1980–89
- College of William and Mary, Williamsburg, Virginia, 1980
- The Johns Hopkins University, Baltimore, Maryland, 1980
- Seton Hall University, South Orange, New Jersey, 1980
- Tuskegee Institute, Tuskegee, Alabama, 1980
- Rensselaer Polytechnic Institute, Troy, New York, 1980

- University of San Diego, San Diego, California, 1980
- Incarnate World College, San Antonio, Texas, 1980
- St. John Fisher College, Rochester, New York, 1981
- Seattle University, Seattle, Washington, 1981
- University of Toledo, Toledo, Ohio, 1981
- Saint Ambrose College, Davenport, Iowa, 1981
- University of Scranton, Scranton, Pennsylvania, 1981
- University of Cincinnati, Cincinnati, Ohio, 1981
- University of Michigan, Ann Arbor, Michigan, 1981
- Hope College, Holland, Michigan, 1981
- University of Brasilia, Brazil, 1981
- New York University, New York, New York, 1982
- Indiana State University, Terre Haute, Indiana, 1982
- Madonna College, Livonia, Michigan, 1982
- Loyola Marymount University, Los Angeles, California, 1982
- Hahnemann Medical College and Hospital, Philadelphia, Pennsylvania, 1982
- Kalamazoo College, Kalamazoo, Michigan, 1982
- Loretto Heights College, Denver, Colorado, 1982

- Universidad Catolica Madre y Maestra, Santo Domingo, Dominican Republic, 1982
- Ramkhamhaeng University, Bangkok, Thailand, 1983 (in absentia)
- Saint Joseph's College, Rensselaer, Indiana, 1983
- Rider College, Trenton, New Jersey, 1983
- Colgate University, Hamilton, New York, 1983
- Immaculate Conception Seminary, Darlington, New Jersey, 1983
- St. Leo's College, St. Leo, Florida, 1984
- West Virginia Wesleyan College, Buckhannon, West Virginia, 1984
- University of Notre Dame, Notre Dame, Indiana, 1984
- Carroll College, Helena, Montana, 1985
- College of Mount St. Joseph, Mount St. Joseph, Ohio, 1985
- Holy Family College, Philadelphia, Pennsylvania, 1985
- Duke University, Durham, North Carolina, 1985
- Christian Brothers College, Memphis, Tennessee, 1985
- St. Thomas University, Fredericton, New Brunswick, 1985
- Walsh College, Canton, Ohio, 1985
- Briar Cliff College, Sioux City, Iowa, 1986
- Aquinas College, Grand Rapids, Michigan, 1986

- University of Nebraska, Lincoln, Nebraska, 1986
- University of Pittsburgh, Pittsburgh, Pennsylvania, 1987
- Universidad Francisco Marroquin, Guatemala la Asuncion, Guatemala, 1987
- University of Malta, Valletta, Malta, 1988
- Rockhurst College, Kansas City, Missouri, 1988
- Wheeling Jesuit College, Wheeling, West Virginia, 1989
- Loyola University, New Orleans, Louisiana, 1989
- Mount Saint Mary's College, Emmitsburg, Maryland, 1989
- Brown University, Providence, Rhode Island, 1989

1990–99
- Loras College, Dubuque, Iowa, 1990
- The Defiance College, Defiance, Ohio, 1990
- Saint Olaf College, Northfield, Minnesota, 1990
- George Washington University, Washington, D.C., 1991
- Our Lady of Holy Cross College, New Orleans, Louisiana, 1991
- Gannon University, Erie, Pennsylvania, 1992
- Mount Mercy College, Cedar Rapids, Iowa, 1993

• Notre Dame College, Manchester, New Hampshire, 1993
• Wake Forest University, Winston-Salem, North Carolina, 1993
• Marian College, Indianapolis, Indiana, 1994
• Avila College, Kansas City, Missouri, 1994
• North Park College, Chicago, Illinois, 1995
• Saint Vincent College, Latrobe, Pennsylvania, 1996
• College of Saint Francis, Joliet, Illinois, 1996
• Albertus Magnus College, New Haven, Connecticut, 1996
• University of Notre Dame Australia, Fremantle, Australia, 1997
• The College of Saint Rose, Albany, New York, 1997
• The University of Kentucky, Lexington, Kentucky, 1998
• Touro College Law Center, Huntington, New York, 1998
• Barry University, Miami Shores, Florida, 1998
• State University of New York, Institute of Technology at Utica/Rome, New York, 1999
• Connecticut College, New London, Connecticut, 1999

2000–02
• University of Saint Francis, Fort Wayne, Indiana, 2000
• Holy Cross College, Notre Dame, Indiana,

2000

• Saint Peter's College, Jersey City, New Jersey, 2000

• North Carolina State University, Raleigh, North Carolina, 2000

• St. Edward's University, Austin, Texas, 2001

• Georgian Court College, Lakewood, New Jersey, 2001

• Ohio State University, Columbus, Ohio, 2002

• Ivy Tech State College, South Bend, Indiana, 2002

• University of San Diego, San Diego, California, 2002